The End of Democracy?

Richard Thorne

Copyright © 2014 Richard Thorne

All rights reserved.

ISBN: 9781494969943

DEDICATION

I dedicate this book to those at the margins of our society;
living at the edge of survival in a world of plenty.

It Is Time For Change.

CONTENTS

	Acknowledgments	I
1	Introduction	1
2	System Failure	16
3	Living on the Edge	31
4	Zombie Nation	63
5	True Democracy	77
	Endnotes	88

Rajni,

Let's Believe in Better!

RT

ACKNOWLEDGMENTS

I would like to thank all those who have supported me in conceptualizing, writing and publishing this book. You know who you are and I am indebted to you.

1 INTRODUCTION

True Democracy
Two thousand, five hundred years ago in a corner of the Mediterranean Sea, a city was experimenting with a new form of government. Athens, a city state of several hundred thousand people had developed a form of democracy that is arguably far more radical than any system of democracy that we have today. There were no kings, queens, prime ministers or presidents. Their governing assembles, parliament and courts were not filled by career politicians and lawyers; they were filled by the public in their thousands.

Athens gave us the word democracy (literally translated as "people power") and for them it really did mean people power. The public took responsibility for their own governance and those who qualified as fully fledged citizens[1] would vote on the creation of laws or participate in carrying out justice. The system of democracy meant that anyone could propose new laws or decisions. Even the civil servants were elected from among the public or chosen at random using a lottery.

Fast forward thousands of years to the 21st century and "people power" appears to be experiencing something of a renaissance. The US elected its first black president; dictatorships across the world have fallen like dominoes in the face of popular uprisings from Tunisia all the way through to Myanmar. Most of the former communist states have shaken off their tyrants and the European Union continues to bring former soviet states into the fold of democratic nations. Even in the midst of the greatest economic crisis since the great depression, we have seen nothing like the rise of autocratic communist and fascist movements that blighted much of the 20th century. It appears obvious that there is an unstoppable and global forward march toward democracy. It is surely only a matter of *when* not *if* the few remaining dictators and autocrats are swept away forever.

Yet there is something wrong with this picture. Under scrutiny, the future of democracy is actually rather more fragile than it may first appear. For a start, hardly anyone actually lives even lives in a functioning democracy. In fact, just 10% of the world's population was classed as living within a "full democracy" by The Economist in 2013. Moreover, the process of democratisation seems to have stalled, with the proportion of people living within a full democracy largely unchanged over the last few years.[2] In other words, despite all the progress that has been made since the defeat of fascism and communism, the vast bulk of humanity still has little or no say in the way that they were governed.

And what about the lucky few people that live in a country blessed with a full democracy? By having this as the very top band of the democratic scale, it is implied that this is as good as democracy gets. Most of Europe and North America fall into this category along with a smattering of other countries around the world like Australia and Japan.

THE END OF DEMOCRACY?

All these countries practice a representative brand of governance, whereby once every four or five years the electorate choose a set of career politicians to govern the country on their behalf.

However, this brand of democracy is far from being *truly* democratic. In stark contrast to the Athenian model, it is a system that allows the electorate only strictly limited and controlled input into their governance as one of a whole number of influencing actors. The electorate is barred from getting too involved in government decisions and can only provide the vaguest steer as to direction they would like to see their country take. The reality is that the population is confined to voting for a very limited handful of political parties, often with little difference between them. Depending on what the election is or where they live, they may be restricted to a choice of just two political parties to choose from and get this opportunity about a dozen times during their whole life time.

The public certainly do not have a vote on individual policies (except on rare occasions, such as Scotland's independence referendum). When different political parties share common policies, there is little scope at all for the public to oppose them. If for example, the two main political parties wanted to support a war, or raise taxes, how does the electorate stop them through the ballot box? They cannot. The electorate votes on a whole manifesto, not on individual elements. If most of the policies of political party are palatable, they may get elected despite no public support for their other policies.

When you really think about it, how much influence do you think that you have over your own government? If we were to pick a model of democratic best practice, surely the US and UK would have to be up there right? Certainly, the politicians of these two countries constantly talk up their role as exporters of "freedom" and "democracy" to the world. However, what brand of democracy are they benevolently trying to pitch to the globe? When you take a machete to the hubris, you find that the US and UK elected governments have taken power with barely any public support at all. When you talk to the voters, you find an electorate totally disillusioned and disengaged with politics. Either they don't vote or they vote begrudgingly from the meagre selection before them. Voters don't really believe they have a choice and that's a real problem. It means that so called "full democracy" is not what it's cracked up to be.

It gets worse. The electorate is by no means the only show in town. For a start, the party that gets into power already has its own agenda. That agenda is influenced but not created by the electorate; it does not emerge from the grassroots. It is in fact developed from above by the political party's own internal machinery and think-tanks. The electorate by contrast is a challenge or barrier to be overcome on the way for the party to achieve its goals. We are a group to be convinced and cajoled using the full power of modern marketing and behaviour change techniques.

Politicians are themselves generally unrepresentative of the population they purport to represent and are very likely to have come from privileged backgrounds or political dynasties that are predisposed to furthering the narrow interests of the party. In the UK for example, it is estimated that a third of members of parliament went to fee paying private schools (compared with a national average of only 7%).[3] In the US, over half the Congress is populated with millionaires.[4] The unrepresentative nature of government is a common theme across the full democracies.

THE END OF DEMOCRACY?

Another key influencing factor is the awesome fire-power of the lobbyists that access and influence government on behalf of their fee-paying clients. Below the radar of public awareness, these thousands of lobbyists vie to influence the government to promote the interests of business and other agendas. In the UK the professional lobbying industry is big business and in 2007 was estimated to be worth £1.9billion ($3.1billion), employing a vast army of 14,000 people.[5] Elected politicians are approached hundreds of times a day, every day by lobbyists. In the US, the scale of lobbying is ten times bigger. In 2011, one estimate of overall lobbying spending nationally was well over $30billion dollars![6] How can a vote by the electorate once every four or five years possibly compete with that? Access to government should not be about who has the biggest wallet, if it is, then People Power is dead. Democracy is dead.

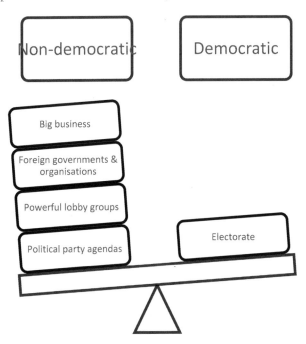

Our government is not just influenced by powerful forces within our borders. It is also under the enormous influence of a powerful and undemocratic force that I call "International Homogeny." This is reflected in the ever growing concentration of power in the hands of a small cluster of international and undemocratic organisations. This is not a new force *per se;* it has been centuries in the making. International governance first emerged as force at the peak of the European empires, in particular those of France and the United Kingdom. A key aspect of these empires was to homogenise everything from language and culture to law and religion. However, the overriding purpose of these empires was to generate even more wealth for the elite of those countries through the opening up of trade and the imposition of the European monetary systems.

While it appeared superficially that, the European empires faded away after the second half of the 20th century and that their colonies became autonomous; this would be a gross misrepresentation of reality. If anything, the process of homogenisation went into overdrive. Unless the colonies flocked to the banner of another brand of homogony - international Communism – they continued to 'westernise' on every level from their law and monetary systems to their culture and habits of consumption as exemplified through the remarkable rise of global brands such as McDonalds and Coca Cola.

It was big business that drove the European policies of the last century, and it is big business that is now driving the current internationalism. This influence is so potent that its effect is to stifle the influence of citizens on the decision making of their own governments. How many Afghanis, Pakistanis, Yeminis, Cubans or Iraqis want American troops or drones operating on their territory? The US government outvotes the electorate of these

THE END OF DEMOCRACY?

countries every time.

The power of the US government is vast. In July 2013, we saw an illustrative example of this power being exerted, not on small countries but on some of the most powerful global economies. On direct orders from Washington, European countries and so called "full democracies," one-by-one broke international law and conventions to deny airspace to the President of Bolivia on suspicion that his private jet contained the whistle-blower Edward Snowdon. In a shocking breach of international diplomatic protocols, the aircraft was forced to land in Austria and was unceremoniously searched. The intelligence was flawed and Edward Snowdon was nowhere to be found, but very briefly, the veil was lifted to reveal who really pulls the strings.

At what point did the citizens of the USA, France or Germany become involved in these key decisions? These are events being played out above the heads of the public on a constant basis. National governments and international organisations see the electorate as obstacles to be overcome and not masters of the process. Do you feel that the German people, the American people, or the Zambians came up with the policies of the International Monetary Fund (IMF) or the World Bank? There is a severe shortage of democracy at the national level and complete absence of democracy at the hugely powerful international organisations that impact so heavily not only our lives today but on the direction of the world as a whole.

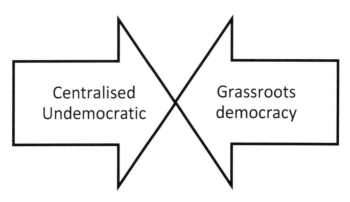

Yet when the quest for true democracy seems hopeless, a second and opposing force has unleashed itself on the world stage. This force is only just coming into its own but has done so on a shockingly rapid and unpredictable scale. This second force is the spontaneous mass mobilisation of populations that rise up against their governments, whether they are dictatorships as in Libya and Tunisia or "elected" governments such as Brazil and Turkey. Sweeping away governments and institutions, these forces have temporarily upset the old order. These uprisings have differed from those in the past insofar as they are self-organising and leaderless, co-ordinated through social media such as Twitter. So stunned by the strength of the uprising in Turkey's cities against his autocratic policies, President Recep Erdogan infamously declared that *'social media is the worst menace to society.'*

Like so-called democracies around the world, Erdogan sees popular engagement with democracy as being a once in five-year's type of affair. I believe that he is wrong. The political classes are wrong to broad-brush governments as "democracies" or "dictatorships." So called democracies in the 21st century are often far from that. Even in established democracies such as the UK and USA, vast numbers of people refuse to vote and even those who do, believe that they have little real choice between the candidates that they are choosing from. Established democracies have become elitist, incestuous and inaccessible to the population at large.

When a government no longer reflects the will of the people, when it takes on a life of its own, it becomes tyrannical. Today governments act as manipulators and propagandists, nudging and coercing their populations while locking them out of the key decision making.

The recent scandalous behaviour of western intelligence services in their mass surveillance of their own populations, all without the consent of the voting citizens is demonstrative of a government out of control and distant from the will of their people. Unchecked we will continue to have global policy making being decided without any input from the vast majority.

Pathway to Utopia
The term "utopia" was first coined by the English lawyer and parliamentarian Sir Thomas More in a book he published in 1516.[7] He created the word by combining the Greek words *eu* (good), *ou* (not) and *topos* (place) to describe a perfect but imaginary island in the Atlantic Ocean. The inhabitants of this fictional land lived within what he regarded as an ideal human society which had no war, injustice or inequality. On Utopia, there was equality between men and women (by the standards of his age), education for all and its citizens were happy and content in a communal arrangement where nobody owned private property.

Utopia was a truly visionary idea created by one of the most influential and respected figures of his time. The Dutch humanist Erasmus, a contemporary of More declared him to be a person *'whose soul was more pure than any snow, whose genius was such that England never had and never again will have its like.'* He was clearly a brave man too, for his writing was satirical and subversive. It was a stab at the tyranny and unfairness he saw around him; as embodied in particular by King Henry VIII. Infamous for his succession of six wives (two of which he had executed), the king also squandered the fortunes that he had inherited from his father on palaces and ostentatious displays of wealth.

Desperately short of funds and furious that the Pope would not allow him to divorce his first wife, the king seized the vast wealth of the Catholic Church and crowned himself the head of a new *English* Christian protestant religion. The Church of England was born and to this day, the British monarchy is the official head of this religion. [8] England in the 16th century was still largely organised within a feudal system that put power firmly in the hands of a tiny and all-powerful elite. Feudalism worked through a system whereby most of the land was concentrated in the hands of a small number of powerful barons, the Church and the king. Land was leased from these all powerful land owners by lesser barons who in turn parcelled out and leased land to lower ranking members of society and so on. At the bottom of the pile was the vast majority of the population that comprised the peasant classes, or 'serfs' that had no land[9] or property and little recourse to justice. They were destined to be trapped in poverty and had little freedom; bonded as they were to their landlords, living like slaves and having limited power to choose where and how they lived or worked.

At one time in favour with Henry VIII, who knighted him for services to the crown; Sir Thomas More was ultimately executed for his refusal to accept the King as the supreme head of the new English Church. Despite his untimely demise, his book was a hit throughout Europe and the term "utopia" would eventually become adopted in languages all around the world. It has since come to describe more generally the concept of a perfect or idealistic model of human existence. The 'American Dream', soviet communism or a kibbutz could all be described as utopian concepts, even if the *reality* doesn't quite meet the *aspiration*. What person hasn't dreamed of having a better life? The same is true for a person living in poverty at the margins of society as it is for someone with a secure job and a comfortable life. To imagine a better way of living is to be human, it has driven us to achieve the vast progress that we have made in the brief time that we have been on this planet.

For most of us in the developed world, life is relatively comfortable. We have a huge degree of freedom and choice. We are relatively safe and secure within stable countries. Welfare budgets provide us with a safety net if we fall ill or lose our jobs. Our lives are far easier than those of our parents or their parents before them. Despite a few bumps along the way, we seem to be on an unerring trajectory to an ever brighter future delivered to us in large part through the redistribution of low skilled jobs to developing countries, phenomenal advances in technology and the industrial scale exploitation of our planetary resources. We can dare to dream that we are in the process of fabricating a utopia here on Earth.

However, the assumption of a progressively better future for humanity is misguided. Utopia has a dark and evil twin – dystopia. Being the polar opposite of utopia, the term describes a world of fear and misery. This is unfortunately the reality for many people all over the world. Despotic dictators rule countries like North Korea and Belarus. Elsewhere a lack of any cohesive governance leads to a lawless and chaotic society where a fearful people have no recourse to justice from armed thugs, criminals and corrupted officials from Mexico and Somalia to Afghanistan.

Dystopia has plagued humanity past and present. In the not too distant past, the indigenous peoples of north, central and southern America and indeed African Americans have had their own dystopias under white rule. Europe was almost destroyed by fascist dystopias in the first half of the 20th century and in the latter half, a vast swathe of the world was under the grip of soviet communism. It may be hard to imagine, but the seed of each of those dystopias was a utopian dream. Communist idealists sought to end inequality between the social classes, Fascists too sought to provide employment and stability for all their citizens through large scale state intervention. In the Americas, immigrants from Europe, often the poor and marginalised wanted to create a new and better life for themselves and their children, even if it cost the indigenous population their way of life.

This duplicity persists even now. The huge improvement to the quality of living in developed countries through the free market capitalist model has been built upon a dystopia of environmental ruination, resource depletion and the exploitation of borderline slave labour in the developing world. Can it be that the current model of free market capitalism that has delivered so much wealth to the developed world is not a pathway to utopia at all; and that will in fact lead us to the mother of all dystopias? No one can deny that the world has recently been wracked by one crisis after another, on a scale not seen since the Great Depression (which was a product of very free market capitalism). Many of these crises can be directly attributed to the free market capitalist model. This is true for climate change and environmental disaster through to financial collapse, unemployment and the sky-rocketing prices of basic essentials such as food and energy.

THE END OF DEMOCRACY?

We should not underestimate the potential for dystopia to engulf even the developed world because of the failings of the free market capitalist system. Large and powerful civilisations from the Egyptian and Roman empires to the Soviet Union have collapsed before and our current civilisation is no more immune today. In his bestselling and highly acclaimed book "Collapse" Jared Diamond starkly demonstrates how past civilisations were all but irradiated from the pages of history due to unsustainable growth of the sort generated by the free market capitalist model today.

The collapse of the Easter Islanders came because of over-exploitation of the island's finite resources (an economic and ecosystem failure) in part because of a huge investment in massive stone monuments. By cutting down all their trees (largely to transport and erect the famous stone heads), they were left without a vital resource with which to build homes or fishing vessels. The loss of trees not only prevented fishing but was devastating to agriculture; causing the rich soil to be washed away and providing no shelter from the wind and the relentless sun. Crops failed, the population starved, the leaders were overthrown and the island descended into anarchy. War and starvation lead to a collapse in the population and by the time that Captain Cook "discovered" the islands in 1770 the civilisation was reduced to a tiny handful of desperate people, rife with stories of cannibalism and desperate to escape the dystopian hell they had unwittingly created for themselves.[10]

There is a real and growing risk that our current individualistic and profit-driven economic model is ushering even the developed world into an imminent dystopian future. Instead of seeking radical new approaches, the international financial institutions and power brokers of the world are advocating yet more of the same flawed free market capitalism. This is coupled with the requirement for crippling austerity measures that threaten to break the back of developed countries and ruin developing countries.

So powerful is the yearning for a better life and yet so elusive, that we have long ago forged a coping strategy. That strategy is called the *afterlife*. Our dreams may seem unachievable on Earth, but perhaps then they could be fulfilled after we have perished? Across the world and throughout history, people have placed their aspirations for a better life on the belief in a utopian paradise that they will enter upon death. The concept is at the heart of religion the world over and taken to extremis can lead to an ambivalent or fatalistic attitude to building an ideal life here on Earth. The abbot leading the pope's army in the bloody massacre of 20,000 men, women and children of the French city of Beziers in 1209 infamously said *'Kill them all, God will know His own.'* Thereby employing a twisted logic that murder was ok, because God would take care of those who were loyal to him in the afterlife. Unfortunately, it is a logic still employed by fundamentalists today; a suicide bomber will indiscriminately blow up a market place in Iraq or a train in Spain causing hell on Earth while believing fervently that a wonderful afterlife awaits those who deserve it.

I believe that the global economic and environmental crisis is an opportunity for the citizens and leaders of the world to stand back, reassess their current socio-economic models, and really think what it is that we are all striving to achieve and at what human and environmental cost. Is unsustainable economic growth as advocated by the free market capitalist model the only way? Is deregulation and large global corporations the answer? Is the growing gulf between rich and poor, within countries and between countries truly desirable? Should profit be the prime motivator for the progress of humanity? Is an illusionary democratic system where the agenda is driven by the few, as good as it gets? Like Sir Thomas More, centuries before me, I would like to believe that there is another way. Humanity is endowed with the powerful and creative ability to envision a better world and has the skills and resources to achieve it. Humanity is not the cynical species that economists would describe us, driven by profit and barely controlled greed. We are far more complex than that, with motivations driven by a sense of fulfilment and purpose, love, and a desire to have a useful role in our societies. A better world can only ever be achieved if we harness the best parts of our nature and not the very worst. A future will only be secured through the collective and unified endeavour of the majority, with the wellbeing of humanity and the biosphere and not monetary profit at its heart. Equality can only be achieved when the majority are fully engaged with the running of their country.

2 SYSTEM FAILURE

Century in crisis
In the run up to the 21st century, governments on every continent dug deep into public funds to build a "legacy" of follies and put on dazzling firework displays.

Yet for all the hubris of the New Millennium celebrations, one could genuinely look with well founded optimism to a future of growth and prosperity. A future where not just the developed countries; but also poorer nations, would share in the wealth of an increasingly interconnected and technologically sophisticated world. Already there had been unprecedented growth in the newly emerging economies of Eastern Europe, Asia and South America, following vast flows of investment from the developed West. It was anticipated that within the first quarter of the 21st century these fast-developing countries would take their place as developed countries.

Poorer countries were growing far quicker than richer ones and the proportion of people in poverty was on a sharp downward trend. New great powers such as Brazil, India, Indonesia and China were about to take their rightful place at all the top tables on the world stage.

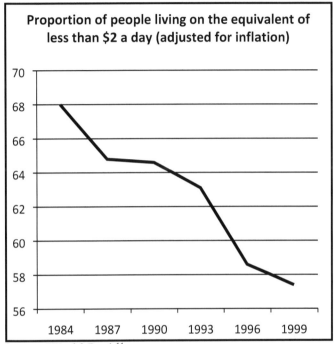

Source: World Bank[11]

The world had emerged from the Cold War that had ended just a few years before in 1991 and with it the constant and very real threat of a third world war and a global nuclear holocaust. With the abrupt collapse of the Soviet Union, there was born a New World Order (NWO), dominated by just one unrivalled superpower and one economic model. Dozens of ex-communist countries were in the process of transforming into fully fledged democratic capitalist states. Eastern Europe was shedding its image as the impoverished relative of Western Europe. George W. Bush's administration would later refer to the region as "New Europe," with a youthful, hard working and highly educated, yet cheap population.

RICHARD THORNE

The latter half of the 20th Century saw the ascent of global capitalist hegemony. Under this NWO, there would be a single dominant and global economic system, based on the US free market model. From an economic perspective, world leaders touted the NWO as a positive thing, providing a peaceful, stable platform for trade and business dealings, allowing companies to more easily operate across country borders.

During the Cold War, the USA and her allies spent billions of dollars undertaking overt and covert operations to spread its economic model to all the peoples of the world. Democracy was always a secondary objective, right behind allowing US companies to access markets and do business. Time and time again, the USA and her allies have supported dictatorships and unelected leaders because they fallen in line with the global capitalist system, even to the extent of helping to topple democratically elected leaders that have threatened to boot out foreign companies.

Even after the fall of communism, this policy of rewarding regimes that are open for business and punishing those that aren't is still being pursued. This is one of the reasons why communist Cuba is crippled by sanctions and communist China is given the red carpet. Democracy and basic human rights are not an essential pre-requisite to being a part of the NWO. Saudi Arabia, The United Arab Emirates, China and Yemen are a testament to this reality.

Whatever your view of the NWO, there would is no room for any other system of society, as the nations of the world transformed their economies to align with the global capitalist model. At the start of the 20th century, Britain had passed the reigns of financial hegemony to the USA and by the end of the century; even China had quietly ceded defeat and has swiftly taken its place in the international hegemony of the NWO as the "workshop of the world." By the beginning of the 21st century, the integration of economies around the world was nearing completion under globally agreed systems of finance, law and trade. Projects such as the European Union (EU) demonstrated just how far this integration could go. Fiercely independent countries with long histories of rivalry and conflict with different languages and cultures somehow overcame these differences and gave up a measure of their independence to join in political and economic union. The EU facilitated the free movement of people, goods and services within its borders and homogenised law and regulations across member countries. For most of its members it also involved the membership of a new single currency imaginatively called the "Euro" which is an enormous step considering both the historic significance of the replaced currencies and sacrifice of national sovereignty over monetary policy.

Each of the 27 member states has to adopt EU laws and obey the rulings of EU law courts over their own national courts of law. For example, a ruling by the European Court of Human Rights prevented the UK from extraditing the illegal immigrant and Europe's leading Al Qaeda terrorist suspect; Abu Qatada back to his home country of Jordon, because he may not have a fair trial. The USA has been a strong supporter of the EU project and has long pressurised the member states to include even more countries, such as Turkey, within the club.

Similar economic and political unions are developing all over the world, meaning that most of the world's population is now part of one or another union. These include the Association of South East Asian Nations covering South East Asia, the North American Free Trade Agreement covering North America, Commonwealth of Independent States comprising Russia and neighbouring countries, the African Union and the Arab Union among others. Where the EU has led, others are following on their way toward the NWO of global homogenisation that is critical to an efficient global capitalist system and the process of doing business.

At the turn of the century there were no regimes left to threaten the way of life that the populations of the democratic capitalist nations of the world had grown accustomed. In contrast to the Soviet Union, the awaking giant of communist China appeared to have no interest in aggressively exporting its brand of socialism and was far more interested in joining international institutions and integrating into the capitalist economic machinery. States like North Korea and Afghanistan were almost irrelevant anomalies that would surely have their time. Terrorism was a blight only afflicting failed states and developing countries.

The UK under the "New Labour" partnership of Tony Blair and Gordon Brown was booming. In 1997, the party swept to power in a landslide victory. Their theme song *'Things can only get better'*[2] reflected the mood of a nation roaring back from a long period lack-lustre economic growth and a divisive Conservative government led by John Major. Under Tony Blair's premiership an intense period of negotiations resulted in the end of decades of republican and unionist terrorist activities in Northern Ireland and the historically momentous start of power-sharing at Stormont. This ended the threat of Irish terror attacks in the UK for the first time in generations and gave hope to a future of a more peaceful and fairer society in Northern Ireland.

Under the New Labour leadership, unemployment in the UK plunged to record lows. New schools, hospitals and transport infrastructure were being built and national debt was being paid off. Fuelled in part by public spending and a thriving banking and service sector, the UK was a country feeling more confident about its place in the world. The New Labour government aggressively pursued foreign policy around the world including a series of military action against dictatorships. Their interventions in Sierra Leone, Serbia, Iraq and Afghanistan would become known as "Blair's Wars." The Labour administration confidently invested in a host of expensive new military technologies including two new "super" aircraft carriers for the Royal Navy. Each amongst the largest vessels in the world, they represented a colossal reversal in the historic decline of the UK's navy and symbolised a nation once again assertive in foreign affairs.

The upbeat mood was reflected across the Atlantic. At his millennium celebration address at the end of 1999, Bill Clinton said *'Never before have we had such an opportunity to move toward what the generations have prayed for, peace on Earth and a better life for all. We must both imagine a brighter future and dedicate ourselves to building it, and I ask you all here today to reaffirm the clear understanding that we must do it together... The forces of science, technology, and globalization have shattered the boundaries of possibility, and in the new century, our achievements will be bounded mostly by the limits on our own imagination, understanding, and wisdom.'*[13]

However, it was not long before these optimistic expectations started to unravel and with them the hopes and dreams of a global generation. Three months into the 2000 and the "dotcom" bubble finally burst, wiping billions from global stock markets as widely over-inflated technology shares collapsed. Just a year later, a new global enemy of the NWO exploded onto the scene in spectacular style. The hijacking of four passenger airplanes by Islamic terrorists on 11th September 2001 would fundamentally change the world and trigger several messy wars that remain unresolved. It did not take long before the beginning of the century would become a key milestone in our global human history for all the wrong reasons. In the last 14 years, we have been shaken by one great global crisis after another, which has left many of us fearful and less certain about the future. Whilst some of these crises have been natural disasters, many of the greatest catastrophes were well and truly human-made. Terrorism, military conflict, economic meltdown, the credit crunch, global warming and shortages of the essential commodities of water, food, fuel and raw materials are the ingredients for a perfect storm that is engulfing the world as I write.

The global capitalist system that has been the engine powering the phenomenal economic and technological growth is faltering. Instead of more wealth for all, living standards are plummeting. In the most developed countries, wages have been stagnant or cut, while inflation has been high; steadily eroding incomes. Across the developed world, the average person in 2014 is still financially worse off than the average person in 2008, and will be for years to come. Unemployment has hit new highs all over the developed world. The jobs that do exist demand more and pay less. Full time permanent contracts have been replaced with part time temporary contracts, often and controversially with zero guaranteed hours.

The situation is particularly severe for young people, graduating with expensive degrees but with no jobs to go to. Youth unemployment is an epidemic afflicting many countries across the world from North America and Europe to North Africa and the Middle East. They are referred to in the media as the "lost generation." However, it is upon the shoulders of this disaffected and marginalised generation that the governments of the world are placing our enormous debts. Those who can get work often have to accept low paid, low skilled and part time jobs. A report by the International Labour Organisation (ILO) states that the effects of youth employment generate *"current discomfort (from unemployment, underemployment, and the stress and social hazards associated with joblessness and prolonged inactivity), but also possible longer term consequences in terms of lower future wages and distrust of the political and economic system. It is exactly the latter consequence that has come to play as one aspect of the Arab Spring."*[14]

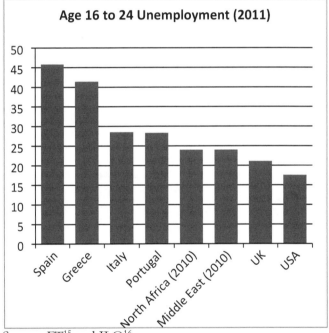

Source: FT[15] and ILO[16]

Whilst the change in fortunes is coming as a complete shock to the developed world, the situation is far worse in the poorest swathes of our shared planet. More than one billion people end each day starving and malnourished, wondering where their next meal may come from.

In the depths of this economic meltdown, one would hope that at least prices would fall, but in fact, the opposite is true. Food and fuel prices are still sky-rocketing, taking an ever greater slice from people's dwindling pay packets. No country is immune. In the UK, which is one of the world's richest economies, 1 in 5 people were judged by the government to be in fuel poverty in 2010. By 2011, this number had leapt to 1 in 4 people and the government predicts that the figure will reach 1 in 3 by 2014.[17] Many of those people are now in-debt to their energy suppliers, unable to afford their bills.

There are rapidly growing cracks in the very foundations of our collective societies, just as great civilisations have collapsed in the past, often taking their leaders and populations by surprise, so too our civilisation teeters at the precipice. If you are fortunate enough to reside in a developed country, you will only now be truly feeling the tremors of the failing global economy. Today it is those many hundreds of millions of people subsisting and dying on the margins of our global society, which are bearing the brunt of the unfolding tragedy. Tomorrow it may be our turn.

Even during the so called "good times" of economic prosperity which ended before 2008, the very poorest people were dying at a rate of 25,000 a day from starvation alone. The World Bank estimated that in 2008, 1.29 billion people were living in "absolute poverty," meaning that they were in a state of severe deprivation of basic human needs such as food and water. Of these, about 400 million people in absolute poverty lived in India and 173 million people in China.[18]

The reality is that despite the rapid growth in the global economy; at least half the world's six billion population lived in abject poverty on less than US$2.50 a day, barely able to feed or clothe themselves and their families. In fact, the vast majority of the world dwells in smothering poverty, with 80% of the global population earning less than US$10 a day.[19] Whilst it is true that the standard of living is cheaper in the poorest nations, increasingly the price of even essential items is traded on a global level. As part of the global capitalist system, rich and poor nations alike compete for the exactly the same resources (such as wheat, pork, oil and copper) which are traded globally. Profiting from this starvation and misery are speculators and commodity traders from London to Shanghai who trade in billions of dollars of the produce that people need to survive, forcing prices up or down as they gamble electronically on commodities that they never see or physically own.

The poorest people needing bread to survive have to compete not only with consumers in richer countries and commodity traders, but also cattle. The production of cattle, increasingly popular with the growing middle classes of the developing world (such as China), requires vast amounts of grain. This problem has been exacerbated many times further by the trend toward growing crops to be used as bio fuels. The use of food crops for generating bio fuels to power petrol engines was identified as being one of the key forces behind the rapid rise in grain prices in 2008 that sparked global food riots. Despite bio fuels being recognised as being instrumental in the rise of grain prices, the trend is toward ever more bio fuel production. Countries like Brazil are utterly dependant on bio fuels to power their vehicles. Other major consumers such as the European Union have set targets for its increased use and the USA has worked hard to boost production levels to compete with Brazil.

The rapidly expanding global economy is also a disaster in

other ways, as not only people, but also our environment has been raped, pillaged and destroyed with industrial efficiency. This has led to a massive depletion of irreplaceable and finite resources, substantial damage to our environment and the mass extinction of countless species. The rapid rise of developing economies stimulated by western capitalism has been hailed as a great achievement of our modern times, but in reality, this change has occurred at completely unsustainable rates resulting from insatiable demands for every kind of natural resource.

Before the industrial revolution of the 19th century, the global population stood at well under a billion people. This is probably the most that our planet could probably sustain without the availability of cheap oil. Today the population has increased to almost seven billion people. By 2025 the population is projected to reach eight billion.[20] The only way we could sustain this increase in people has been through an increasingly efficient system of agriculture and resource extraction. However, this ruthless efficiency has hastened the point in time when our resources have been exhausted and are eventually insufficient to meet the burgeoning population needs. We have just set the scene for the mother of all human made calamities.

At the beginning of industrialisation, this was fine as supply easily outstripped demand. Prices of everything from food and clothes to electronics plummeted. Living standards across the world started to rise faster than ever. In the developed world, we have created a generation of excess; goods are so cheap that they became disposable. Once technology breaks or became "out of date" it is simply thrown away and replaced. Clothes could be bought for a few dollars, designed to be worn just a handful of times. Even food is thrown away in vast amounts. The EU infamously bought and stockpiled lakes of wine and mountains of butter to prop up its farmers, before eventually dumping it on the global market or destroying it. Consumers were just as wasteful. A survey in 2008 showed that £10.2 billion ($15.7 billion) of untouched food was thrown away each year in the UK alone.[21] In the USA, a recent study has shown that approximately 40% of food is discarded by consumers.[22]

Unfortunately, this "golden age" of gluttonous excess is coming to its inevitable end. The relentless and insatiable growth in demand has steadily caught up with a dwindling supply of energy, land for food and almost all other commodities. The fact is simply that a growth-based economy does not fundamentally make sense. The reality is that there are only *finite* resources. It should be obvious that if there is only a limited amount of a resource, it needs to be carefully rationed and that a high premium should be placed on using it.

The global capitalist system not only extracts and uses these irreplaceable commodities as fast as possible, but also pays a fraction of their real worth. That is until it's too late and prices suddenly explode, snatching wealth away from the population. This is exactly what is happening today and not only in the poorest parts of the world. In the UK, real income of the middle classes has fallen by approximately £5,300 ($8,630) in the five years since 2008.[23]

The capitalist system actively encourages countries and businesses to compete with other to get commodities and resources quicker and cheaper, or risk losing out to each other. Whilst in the short run, this appears to be a good strategy, in the longer term it is ruinous. Take for example a seafood company which made its shareholders richer and gave customers cheaper prices because it used increasingly bigger boats to catch fish. It is good times for all at the start. Who isn't happier about paying less? In the longer run, it leads to catastrophe. Global fish stocks are currently heading for collapse due to over-fishing. Profits shrink as ships need to be even bigger and travel further for smaller catches and the extra costs mean most of the customers, who previously enjoyed cheap prices, can suddenly no longer afford fish. It is a boom and bust approach.

The example of over-fishing is just one of the multitudes of environmental catastrophes facing us today. In theory, if coordinated global action on fishing is taken *right now*, then we may still have a chance of rebuilding global fish stocks in a process that at best would take generations. Whilst there may still be time to halt the global fish crisis, it is simply not possible to replenish other resources that we rely so heavily upon.

Cheap oil and gas are critical to our economy and our civilisation would literally collapse without them. Rising oil and gas prices are not just an inconvenience they represent a reversal of our economic progress. Economies *will* collapse, people *will* be impoverished and lives *will* be lost.

Yet, just as with fish and many other resources that we will deplete in this half of the 21st century; oil and gas resources are being extracted as quickly as we can possibly get them. The trouble is that these resources, once exploited will never recover, once they are gone the age of *cheap* energy and the world, as we know it is over.

This is why at the start of the 21st century the world economy finds itself nose-diving. In 2008, the world was shaken by the global banking crises and practically overnight trillions of dollars were wiped from the global economy. Around the world, debt-ridden nations had to rescue the banks or see the very pillars of global capitalism and the NWO turn to dust. This unprecedented intervention has brought nations to the brink of bankruptcy and led to emergency austerity budgets across the developed world leading to surging unemployment; pay freezes and a debt burden that will be carried on for future generations long after all of us are gone. The last time things were this bad, democracy was almost snuffed out but this time around, there is no cheap energy to bail us out.

A result of rising energy costs mean that despite a global economic crisis that is the worst since the Great Depression, prices of everything are still increasing relentlessly year on year. Now instead of getting better off, the vast majority of the world is getting poorer and less able to pay their debts and the debts of their governments. This has sparked riots and even regime change across the developing world. The "Arab Spring" was as much to do with falling living standards, as it was to do with democracy. When people are unable to see a better future for them and their families, when people have no work or cannot buy food or clothes, then they have nothing to lose. This is why all over the world violent riots having been taking place. At the extreme end of poverty, tens of thousands of people literally starve to every death *every single day* because they can't afford enough food.

The stage is set for global catastrophe, we can expect more riots and war; we can expect a steep rise in poverty, famine and disease. India and China will be among the next big nations to be affected. India is already struggling to contain Marxist militias and China now spends far more on its *internal* security than on its military. Like many terrified regimes around the globe, the Chinese government knows that the greatest existential threat comes from its own people. Whilst largely unreported in the media, there have been approximately 100,000 riots and demonstrations across China every year since the start of the 21st century and the number and severity of these are increasing. The last decade has seen major separatist uprisings in both Tibet and Xinjiang (an area with a large Muslim population) that were both brutally suppressed.

In common with all adherents to the global capitalist system, China and India believe that the only way to avoid collapse in their countries is through a sustained high level of growth, ideally at least 8% annually. Chinese economic policy is underpinned by the government's belief that if growth falls below 7% a year, it will herald a political and economic crisis. So instead of applying the brakes, the world is still accelerating toward disaster.

A fundamental flaw with the unregulated global capitalist system is that at its core is the principal of the fulfilment of individualistic material desires that are dislocated from the reality that *we are not just individuals*. We are part of natural and human systems. Every single action we take has an impact on the world around us, on other people and on the environment within which we live. Individualistic material capitalism is founded on a false premise. It is base on a lie. A system that ignores the basic realities of the world around us is ultimately doomed to failure and the cost of that failure will be the biggest humanitarian disaster the world has ever seen.

3 LIVING ON THE EDGE

Thirst
The Earth is parched. Rivers the world over are literally drying up as their sources are being tapped for intensive agriculture, industry and expanding cities. Other water sources are polluted by industry and agriculture. Over the coming years, 40% of the world's population will suffer water stress or scarcity.[24] Almost 2 million children die each year from disease and diarrhoea contracted through unclean water. Although water is often regarded as a renewable resource, in many parts of the world we are taking water at a much faster rate than it can be replaced. This is devastating to our environment which relies on the water cycle that we are draining for consumption, disrupting for electricity production and polluting with industrial waste. It is also deadly for people too, as farms and households can no longer get the water that is necessary for survival. All this has an economic as well as humanitarian and environmental cost. According to the World Health Organisation, the lack of clean water costs the global economy $560billion a year.[25]

In the worst hit areas, people have turned to pumping water from ancient ground aquifers. These water sources can take centuries to be replenished, so they can only be treated as a one-off stop gap. Instead they are often being used as the primary source of water across many parts of the world from South America (Mexico city is literally sinking and its roads and buildings collapsing as the government sucks out the water from under it), to Saudi Arabia (where there are no rivers) and India (often illegally, for agriculture). Sana'a, Yemen's capital city is expected to have just a few years of ground water left before this supply runs completely dry. Yemen's oil supplies are also dwindling, at a time when it needs to invest in expensive new water supplies from the sea. In 2007, the World Bank issued a stark warning for the Middle East and North Africa that the available fresh water per person will be halved by 2050.[26]

Aside from using up the finite supply of water from aquifers, some countries have adopted drastic and unsustainable solutions, investing huge sums of money into desalination plants to turn sea water into drinking water. This now occurs across the Middle East and in other countries such as Spain, Australia and Singapore (which also imports vast amounts of water from Malaysia). The cost of this energy intensive practice is rising all the time in line with global energy prices. Currently Saudi Arabia spends over $3billion[27] a year on extracting fresh water from the sea. A hefty bill that is likely to sky rocket further, in sync with rising energy costs and an ever expanding population. These plants are also vulnerable to natural disasters or terrorist attack. Despite the cost of this water source, sheer desperation has caused its use to increase nine-fold over the last 30 years. There are now over 300 million people dependent on water that has been extracted at great expense from the sea.

The chronic problems were highlighted by the Director General of the World Bank's International Water Management Institute. Colin Chartres said that *'If we don't*

THE END OF DEMOCRACY?

[invest] we will see food crises like the one in 2007 repeated over and over again.' He went on to say that water tables in India and China had fallen catastrophically and that this was merely *'an early warning. If nothing is done, you are going to get an increase in social unrest, migration and a fertile ground for terrorism.*'[28] A report 2010 published in the Nature journal provided a damning assessment of the predicament we are in. The report states that over 80% of the world's population do not have a secure natural water supply and that situation was likely to get worse as water tables drop, populations and developments grow and glaciers melt. The scale of the problem seems hopeless and the report's authors stated that for developing countries *'$800bn per year will be required by 2015 to cover investments in water infrastructure, a target likely to go unmet.'*[29] Already people are being displaced. In Syria, hundreds of thousands of people were forced to move from their homes because of a four-year drought, which dried up crops and deprived homes of adequate water supplies.[30]

China may be a rising super power, but a quarter of its population have to drink water that is contaminated. Drought and poor quality water is a massive headache for a country that needs increasing amounts of water for its cities, industries and agriculture. Water is one of key areas that will start to hold back further Chinese growth. As a sign of just how serious things are getting, the great Yangtze river is experiencing its worst drought for decades, at a time when demand for its waters are many times higher than they were 50 years ago when it was last this bad. A whopping 40% of china's colossal industrial activity is now concentrated in the Yangtze delta and things have got so critical that in the summer of 2011 the government was forced to open the flood gates of the controversial "Three Gorges" reservoir in an attempt to support irrigation and drinking supplies downstream. The trouble is that the reservoir is a key electricity generator and the release of vast amounts of water from the dam will harm its ability to generate energy and supply this key economic area, leading to potentially the worst power shortages in years.[31] The consequences of this will be a crippling economic slowdown in a country that is heavily dependent on vigorous growth for stability.

Hunger
Like water, we are utterly dependent upon food for our survival. In developed countries, people spend about 10-15% of their income on food but in developing countries that figure is a lot higher. For China or Brazil, this figure is closer to 50% of an average person's household income. In Africa, people spend on average 75% of their earnings on food.

Little wonder that civil unrest was widespread in the developing world when food prices last peaked 2008 and then again in 2011. The rising cost of rice led to an explosion of violence from Haiti to the Philippines as people struggled to feed their families. In 2008, countries that previously exported food had to cease export in order to feed their own population, further driving up global prices and depriving governments and farmers of crucial export earnings. In January 2008, India was the first Asian country to ban almost all rice exports and this quickly followed by similar bans right across the region from China and Cambodia to Indonesia and Vietnam. The export bans which swept the region demonstrate just how quickly the panic of soaring food prices can spread and just how terrified regimes are of the impact this will have on their survival.

Burma (Myanmar) has had one of the most brutal and autocratic military regimes in south East Asia. Any opposition is crushed and the key opposition figure head, Aung San Suu Kyi has spent most of her political life under arrest. However, both of the biggest and popular uprisings in Burma (1988 and 2007), would probably not have occurred if it were not for escalating food prices. The junta is well aware of this fact and as dictatorships are being toppled around the world, the regime has started to relax its tight grip on the opposition, freeing political prisoners and organising limited elections.

Food prices and inflation have contributed to the 'Arab spring' riots which were triggered by the police orchestrated murder of a university-educated fruit seller trying to make ends meet in Tunisia. The rapid overthrow of the regime in Tunisia inspired similar movements throughout North Africa and the Middle East where undemocratic regimes are the norm. Egypt's Mubarak administration was the next to fall, followed by Libya's Colonel Gadaffi. The region's undemocratic regimes are responding in different ways; those with the cash (such as Saudi Arabia) are throwing money at their population. Those without the spare money are either embarking on the road to democracy or are fighting a pitched battle with their own citizens, as is the case in Syria and Bahrain.

Not only are global food prices higher, but the financial crisis has meant that countries are less able to deal with them. Across North Africa and the Middle-east, countries had been cutting back on food and fuel subsidies which were simply unsustainable and unaffordable as their populations expanded. At the start of 2012, Nigeria was brought to a standstill by several days of public strikes against the sudden removal of a fuel subsidy that doubled petrol prices overnight. Eventually the government had to reintroduce the subsidy or face ongoing riots. People have tolerated dictatorships and autocratic regimes for decades. However, when their standard of living starts to go into reverse and they cannot feed themselves or their families that is when the flames of revolution spread as rapidly, dangerously and unpredictably as wildfire.

The price of food is causing anxiety amongst regimes across the world. In April 2011, Robert Zoellick, president of the World Bank stated that rising food prices were a *'toxic brew of real pain contributing to social unrest.'* He stated that over the course of the year, another 40 million people had reached the depths of extreme poverty, subsisting on less than $1.25 a day.[32] In China, food prices are monitored closely by the authorities who are attempting to ensure that its citizens are able to afford basic essentials. It knows that the country can only be controlled if it continues its blistering pace of growth and increasing living standards. Should that system falter and people find themselves sinking backward into poverty, then anarchy will surely follow. China knows as well as any government that the food crisis is only going to get worse and instead of relying on its ability to import its way out of trouble by competing on the open market, it is not taking any chances. China is in the process of a colossal global land grab - buying up premium agricultural land all around the world from Africa to Latin America to be used exclusively to feed its own people.

Speculators are one of main factors behind rising food prices, as traders buy and sell vast quantities of grain and pork for profit. Glencore is one of the world's biggest traders in wheat and in 2010 courted controversy when it betted on grain prices to rise while simultaneously urging Russia to impose a grain export ban - triggering a huge increase in the global price of grain, while handing the company with a large profit.[33]

Demand for everything from food to hi-tech goods is constantly growing whilst at the same time our fuel and natural resources are being rapidly depleted. More land is required to grow the food necessary to feed the tens of millions of new mouths every year whilst simultaneously agricultural land is being destroyed to build new houses and other developments. As less productive land is employed to try and feed the masses, so to the risks of bad harvests and famine escalate. This is happening all the time around the world.

There is a simple law that every creature on Earth must obey, or else they will starve. We must burn *less* calories getting food then we gain from the food that we consume. During the agricultural revolution, humans were able to harvest calories more efficiently; generating surpluses that could be stored for leaner years or traded for other goods. Yet, they were never able to break the rule that they had to consume more than they used. Ultimately, food surpluses meant that populations could grow rapidly as they were less vulnerable to seasonal and annual changes in food availability. Even this system has its limitations, as the human population rises and available land for agriculture reaches its limit. Animals that were used to boost agricultural productivity also required their share of the output.

Since the discovery of oil and gas, we have literally turned this law of consumption on its head. Today we spend a whopping *70 calories* of energy for every calorie we obtain from food. Oil and gas is so abundant in energy and so cheap that it has been economically viable to burn far more calories than is actually gained from the food that we eat. Despite this huge expenditure of energy, food has never been so abundant and cheap, particularly in developed countries where people spend just a fraction of their incomes on their groceries. Yet this system also makes us highly reliant on oil and gas which is steadily becoming more expensive as demand rockets and supplies dwindle.

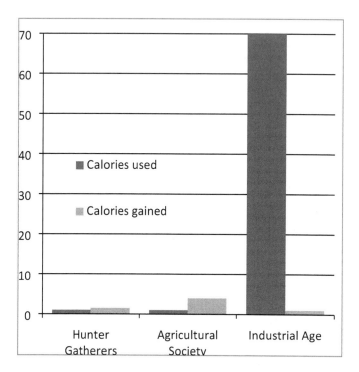

Running on empty

Shortages in reliable food or water supplies are just one interlinked element of the brewing 'perfect storm' which is already threatening to consume us. Despite our technological progress, our currently expanding population is increasingly reliant on the whims of nature. Like addicts we need better crops every year, we need new oil finds, need more commodities of every kind, we need to consume more fresh water than the year before. At the same time, we are poisoning our environment and destroying the resources that we are so dependent upon and contributing to global climate change which is already leading to failed crops and destructive storms. However, the biggest issue above all else is our total reliance on oil and gas.

THE END OF DEMOCRACY?

Oil and gas has been a great one off gift to humanity that has allowed us to spawn the 'Green Revolution' that through the use of gas based fertilizers, agricultural machinery and transport has allowed the world to massively expand food production and feed a growing population. Since this revolution, oil has become an integral part of the process of growing, harvesting and distributing food.

Try and imagine a world without oil, gas, and you would have to imagine a place where every single one of us would be a lot poorer. Even in the developed world, our diet would be very limited, localised and would cost most of our income (as is the case in Africa today). We would rarely travel further than walking or cycling distance. The products and services we take advantage of today from the internet to mobile phones would either not exist or be out of our reach. Health services, education services and all the other services provided by governments would not exist or would be shadow of what they are today. The world around us would look very different, everything from our roads to our cars, mobile phones, clothes and shoes are made of oil. Just try to imagine a world without plastics!

The discovery of oil and gas was like the discovery of a vast army of slaves willing to do our bidding. The amount of oil used to provide just one person in a developed country with food each year is the equivalent to the energy of approximately *100 people*. Only princes of bygone eras could have had the luxury of a hundred slaves and servants to ensure they were well fed.

Before the large-scale exploitation of oil and gas in the latter half of the 20th century, agriculture relied on a system of crop rotation. The meant that the same crop would not be grown on the same field each year and there may also be years with no crops at all. This was designed to put nutrients back into the soil and to make use of different depths of soil at different times of the year. In addition to that, the rotation of crops prevented pests and disease from thriving from year to year.

Today, that system has given way to intensive agricultural production of the same crop year on year, which is made possible through oil and gas based synthetic fertilizers, herbicides and pesticides. The modern agricultural system requires a huge input of energy in return for a high yield of crops able to support much larger populations. Energy is also needed for large scale agricultural machinery such as tractors and combine harvesters. On top of that, food production became global, with food being traded across the globe requiring energy intensive logistical systems to move food which is packaged in oil-based plastic, by truck, boat and air.

Oil and gas is indispensable to our modern living standards and as it is depleted, so to our living standards will reverse. These energy sources simply cannot just be replaced by any existing alternative sources of fuel. Nothing compares to it. It is cheap and easy to extract, store and transport. It does not decay.

Yet the great gift of oil and gas has proved to be a double-edged sword. We are living in a world built and run on oil and gas. Demand is increasing relentlessly as developing nations attempt to replicate the same oil-intensive lifestyles of the developed nations, but global oil supplies are dwindling

The resultant upsurge in oil prices has placed another choke hold on the global economy at the same time that the world is struggling to get out of recession, yoked with great new debts accumulated through supporting our failing banking system. In 2008, the US national debt actually doubled as result of its bailout of American banks. In 2010, US debt was downgraded for the first time in its entire history from its coveted AAA rating to a humiliating AA. Iceland with a GDP of just $13 billion is now saddled with a national debt of $100 billion, which will cripple the local economy and living standards for generations even without enormous burden of the oil crisis. Similarly, the people of Greece, Spain and Italy are in uproar about the sudden and steep reversal in their living standards as the government seeks to keep the countries from bankruptcy.

Whilst oil's contribution to the Green Revolution pushed many people out of hunger poverty, the high price of oil is now reversing these gains and the numbers of people who will starve to death or suffer malnutrition are again on the increase. A report by the United Nation's Food and Agriculture Organisation in 2008 highlights that oil prices have tripled the price of fertiliser and doubled the price of food transportation in the period 2006-08 alone. Simultaneously crops that once were grown to feed people are now being grown to produce 'bio fuels'. In the USA, a third of their corn production is now going to bio fuel production and the World Bank estimates that this practice is one of the leading causes of the surge in global food prices that has plunged an extra 100 million people back into extreme poverty in 2008. The US has recently become the world's largest producer and exporter of bio-fuels, just ahead of Brazil.

Politicians have kept quiet about the energy crisis because they know that to speak truthfully will cause panic in society and on the financial markets which are already battered and beleaguered. The whole economic system we have built is reliant on perpetual growth, which in turn requires the availability of abundant cheap energy. Instead of talking about the fuel crisis, our politicians will talk of climate change and global warming as the reason for all their investment in alternative fuels and targets to reduce energy consumption. The climate change problem is a real one, but it is nowhere near as immediate and urgent as the fuel crisis that is already costing the lives of millions right now.

In 2010, the US military published a report highlighting oil and gas shortages as one of the key threats to the world. The report states that every seven years we will require another Saudi Arabia worth of oil production to meet demand, a prospect that the US military admits is highly unlikely. The report predicts that by 2012 there would be an end to surplus oil production and that *at best* the world economy will have to go through *'periods of harsh economic adjustment.'* [34]

This bleak assessment is reflected by UK business. A report on energy supplies published in 2010 by a taskforce of business leaders including Sir Richard Branson warned that oil supply will potentially peak by 2015 and after that point, supplies will fall rapidly. It predicts that the most likely scenario following this peak in oil supply will be *'a sharp, and permanent, rise in oil prices from which there will be no retreat.'* [35]

Peak oil is the point at which half the known supplies of oil have already been used leaving just half remaining. The trouble is that the remaining half of oil is much more difficult and much more expensive to extract, meaning that when 'peak oil' has been reached it will mark the end of *cheap* oil. The US achieved peak oil production in 1970 and the UK had its own peak oil moment in 1999 when its oil supply started to fall for the first time. In less than 5 years, the UK went from being an oil and gas exporter to an oil and gas importer, following the pattern of the USA and every year the country becomes increasingly reliant on foreign oil and gas.

The world economy doesn't need oil wells to run dry before it disintegrates, the economy will be destroyed well before that point, as growth is choked by ever increasing energy bills. This will drive up inflation making people poorer in every single country. Populations in India and France will both see their living standards fall year after year. It is already happening right now.

Not only are oil supplies peaking, but the countries that control those supplies are looking less stable. Take the world's largest oil producer, Saudi Arabia for example. Its population is young, 40% are under 15 and has high employment at perhaps around 25%. The increasing population has also meant that the living standards have actually started to fall. Falling standards of living are a key precursor to social unrest, especially in countries with a large young population like Saudi Arabia and youth unemployment rates of 30%. This has meant that the government has approved vast increases in social subsides the cost of which can only be met by ever higher oil prices. In 2010, the Saudi government spent $129billion on social programmes, equivalent to half its GDP. Similarly, the Kuwait Government deposited thousands of dollars into the bank accounts of its entire population and promised to allocate them free access to staple foods.[36] This is clearly an unsustainable solution and at some point, these governments will be unable to keep throwing ever larger sums of money at their populations.

The middle-eastern social spending programs include subsidised oil, meaning that domestic consumption of this precious resource is booming. Added to this is the energy required for desalination plants and the building of new industries, means that the oil and gas producing nations of the Middle East are themselves using up the supplies available for export. The United Arab Emirates is already a gas importer and it is estimated that Saudi *domestic* energy demand will increase 250% between now and 2028. This has led to several countries in the region to diversify and start building nuclear power plants including Saudi Arabia. The problems are so large that Qatar is the only country in the region that can meet its own domestic gas demands.[37]

Shortages inevitably cause conflicts and indeed were one of the primary drivers for Japan's entry into the Second World War and subsequent invasion of China. As an agricultural nation, its resource needs were nowhere near as great as when it was transformed into a modern industrial powerhouse. Following the European model, Japan then needed oil, coal and timber to fuel its new industrial economy and war machine. Similarly, China encouraged by the western powers is going through its own rapid process of industrialisation and through this transformation, its appetite for raw materials and fuel is growing on a phenomenal scale.

The South China Sea is an area rich in oil and gas reserves and contains a third of the world's shipping. It is also a vast battleground as competing territorial claims between China, Indonesia, Malaysia, Philippines, Taiwan, Vietnam and Brunei sporadically escalate into skirmishes between rival fleets staking out their claims (often fishing rights) sometimes resulting in casualties. In 2011, Obama recognised this as the next big potential conflict zone and announced an increase in presence of USA forces in South East Asia with new and enhanced bases across the region from Singapore and Australia to the Philippines and Japan. By 2020, the USA will have transferred a massive 60% of their naval forces to the region.[38]

The demand for dwindling oil reserves is a catalyst for conflict as nations compete for control of the remaining oil supplies. This is at least part of the reason why the USA and her allies wholeheartedly supported military campaigns in Iraq and Libya. It is without a doubt that the US and UK oil giants would not now be running some of Iraq's largest oil fields, if Saddam was still in town.

Chasing the Money Changers out of the Temple

In the process of rebuilding the USA after the Great Depression of the 1920's and 1930's, President Franklin D. Roosevelt exclaimed that: *'The money changers have fled from their high seats in the temple of our civilization. We may now restore that temple to the ancient truths. The measure of the restoration lies in the extent to which we apply social values more noble than mere monetary profit.'*

Just like the politicians of today, Roosevelt identified the evil role being played by the bankers and the clear imbalance of the economy in favour of chasing profits over improving society for all. However, far from being hobbled by the government, the financial sector wields more power than ever before. Politicians today threaten to curb the excesses of the financial sector, but this is mere hubris. The reality is that the financial sector is essential for maintaining the free-market capitalist model. Far from punishing banks, Governments have taken tax-payers hard earned money and taken their countries toward bankruptcy in order to support the banks. While banks are helped back to profitability, tax-payers are made to pay more tax and take pay cuts. Meanwhile welfare programmes, universities and pension funds are being raided to support the bank bailouts. During the period between 2008 and 2011, governments all over the world orchestrated a staggering transfer of wealth from their citizens to the banking sector. Like FDR before them, politicians will say whatever it takes to get elected while doing another when they are in office.

Our economic system is failing and for good reason. Free market capitalism is founded on the premise of perpetual growth, which is not a possible concept on a planet with finite resources. Above all, capitalism puts profit making first and foremost, ahead of society and the real needs of humanity. Capitalism is a great tool for extracting resources quickly and efficiently, but it has no palatable answers when those resources are depleted. At the heart of capitalism is a banking system that relies on the perpetual growth model, as banks lend money that they don't have, in the hope that it will be returned several times over in the future. It is because banks have no confidence in the future that lending ground to a halt and the 'credit crunch' has brought the global financial system to its knees since 2008.

The terrifying reality is that the entire basis of our modern civilisation relies on everyone believing in the lie, that the money flowing through our financial systems has a *real* value. When the credit crunch crippled the global economy, trillions of dollars were wiped out. How does such a vast sum of money simply disappear? Where does it go? The fact is that the money didn't go anywhere; it didn't exist in the first place. Even after the credit crunch, the world is playing with 'virtual money' that is not actually anchored to the real world today.

The modern financial system is a product of a vibrant banking system pioneered in Italy and mastered by the great British and Dutch trading nations. When money in the form of coins or paper first appeared in Europe, it was either actually an object of value (such as gold or silver) or a paper note that represented actual objects of value stored safely in a bank vault. However, over time it simply became more convenient to exchange the notes themselves rather than transfer actual gold and silver. Banks used the deposits of silver and gold to lend money in return for interest and over time, they lent more money than they actually had in their vaults. The system worked so long as not everybody wanted their money back at once. Today, money is not actually anchored to anything of value; it relies rather worryingly on *faith* in the system. When that faith goes, so does the value of the money.

In the USA, the Federal Reserve requires that banks keep just 3-10% of their capital, leaving them to lend the rest, which in turn can get deposited in another bank and be lent out again. The reality is that money is 'invented' on a massive scale in the real world, with banks generating vast sums of new money based on the creation and constant recycling of loans, going far beyond the real basis of the wealth. Banks even trade in the debts that they manage, with unscrupulous banks selling off high risk debt to other banks and investors. At some point, someone has to pay for all the ballooning debt. When there is a high risk that the debt can't be repaid it becomes 'toxic', instead of being an asset on a bank's balance sheet, it becomes a liability. This is what brought down the biggest banks all across the world; when so called assets were at a key stroke classified as liabilities and vast sums of virtual money simply 'vanished' from the banking system. Every single country on this planet is spending money it does not have; borrowed from future generations that have not yet been born. The system only works on the flawed hypothesis that the next generation will be richer than the one before, so are able to pay the debts generated today. The problem is that next generation, the young people of today, even in developed countries, are being dubbed the "lost generation," emerging poorer and more debt ridden than their parents before them.

If you need further evidence that money is not actually connected to real wealth, simply observe the recent practices of central banks all around the world as they participate in Quantitative Easing (QE) which is a fancy way of saying *printing money*. Except that money isn't even printed, it is simply electronically typed into a central bank's balance sheet. It seems bizarre that money can be created in this way, but it is common practice for the world's biggest central banks. This invented electronic money is then used to buy government debt or is lent to other banks thereby allowing the government to keep paying its bills and banks to keep functioning long after other banks and private investors have lost faith in them.

As we have seen, banks are essential for the capitalist system as they provide easy access to equity for businesses and individuals to invest in growth or buy goods and services. Because of the credit crunch, banks are far more cautious about who they lend money to, which has had the result of applying the brakes to economy. Banks may lend money, but in order to function effectively they also require equity which they gain from depositors and investors. However, investors have been staying away from banks as they are seen quite rightly as a high risk investment. This has meant that financial institutions have had to pay a premium rate of interest just to get access to investment. This is the same for governments; Germany for example has recently raised money by selling debt at 0% interest as investors became more concerned with putting their money somewhere safe. By contrast, Spain or Greece struggle to raise money at all, and have to pay high premiums that they can barely afford at around 6 or 7%.

This is where QE comes into play. At a key stroke, the central banks can create money which they then use to buy assets, (such as government or banking debt) which has the effect of reducing the interest that governments and banks have to pay to investors. In practice, the financial institutions have happily accepted the central bank's cash but have done little to share that money into the rest of the economy, instead hoarding the money and paying down debts. This has led to central banks all over the world injecting even more invented money into the financial institutions. In the USA, the Federal Reserve created approximately $2.5trillion through QE since 2008. Similarly, the UK's Bank of England generated around $490billion to buy up the debts of the banks and government.

It might seem too good to be true; and it is. By creating additional money, the central bank is in effect devaluing the currency which means that savings are eroded and prices sky-rocket. Hyper-inflation has happened in the past (Germany during the Great Depression) and happens today (Zimbabwe). It can happen again with disastrous consequences. Today China and other Asian economies are busily snapping up the extra dollars, pounds and euros in the system as they try to keep their own currencies low enough to export their products to their main markets. The global economy is reliant on the continued growth of Asia, but that growth cannot be taken for granted as the financial crisis deepens and their main export markets stagnate. What happens when Asia can no longer buy vast quantities of dollars?

Since global economic crisis of 2008, China has ploughed vast amounts of cash into its economy to keep its economy afloat as its exports slumped. In just a few short years, the easy loans provided by the Chinese government had inflated to extraordinary levels. By 2014, its banking sector exposure to debt had reached critical levels on par with the USA in 2008. Chinese government debt has accounted for half of all the $30 trillion increase in world debt over the past five years.

Our unsustainable growth has placed many of the poorest

on the verge of disaster but even in the west, the cost of living is rising, the number of houses being repossessed due to bankruptcy is record breaking, and many tens of millions are losing their jobs. This is just the beginning as the slide into longer term decline was delayed by massive Government spending programs that have bailed out bad banks, helped people buy new cars and invested in new infrastructure projects. This spending has served to put many nations into great debt and developed nations from Iceland to Greece have come close to bankruptcy. At some point, the spending will have to come to an abrupt end as Governments tighten their belts and raise taxes.

Public sector cutbacks will have a negative impact that will ripple out into the wider economy as unemployment rises, peoples spending decreases and those who are still have jobs are burdened with higher taxation. These factors will starve spending on the high street. At best, the world economy will see a slow and painful recovery, but it is far more likely that the coming years will bring further economic woe across the globe. Unlike the Great Depression, there will be no cheap oil to bail us out. Having utterly exploited nature's great gift, we will have to pay the price in full.

One of the attributes of capitalism is that it is dependent on the need for constant growth, if growth slows or stops, the system fails. Employers have to cut production and this increases unemployment that in turn decreases demand and leads to further production cuts which in turn leads to further unemployment. At the same time, wages slow or fall and people generally cut spending. It is a downward spiral that rapidly gets out of control and this is why unfettered capitalism can be so dangerous.

Burden of debt
The fall of communism toward the end of the 20th century

removed the last remaining major obstacle to the dominance of the NWO of global capitalism and free market economics. The ideology of the individual materialist over the communist was shown to be the only show left in town. This ideology is now dominant across the world through the process of freer trade and globalisation all supported by global financial institutions like World Bank and International Monetary Fund.

Globalisation can be seen to be a positive force in the world as it naturally breaks down barriers between nations and the peoples of the world through the promotion of trade in goods, services and culture. Yet let us not be deluded by the fact that globalisation today is not primarily concerned with selflessly unifying peoples, but has evolved as a direct result of being good for business and maximising profits, particularly for the rich and powerful elites. Capitalist countries survive and thrive on the need to facilitate the needs of business as this is the basis for economic performance. The financially richest nations in the world are those that best facilitate the growth of business and promote its interests. The primary interest of government in capitalist nations is to support the economy and business first and foremost. This is not a secret agenda, on the contrary, the nation's population wants to work and be able to fund their individualistic materialistic lifestyles and they recognise the need for their government to support job creation and enterprise.

Can we imagine a developed country without the pre-eminence of business? In the 21st century, we are now trapped in this rat race of reliance on business for all our needs for jobs, for food and for our materialistic goods. Global corporations have no consideration for the long term future or benefit of you, your family and your community. The excesses of business resulted in the massive global crash of the 1920's which spawned great misery and gave birth to tyrants that in turn led to the death and destruction of tens of millions.

Unfortunately, it was inevitable that we would have to endure the mother of all hangovers many times worse than the Great Depression when finally this most recent economic bubble finally burst. Worse is to come as the USA sinks into greater debt year on year funded by the equally fragile economies of China and India. Western debt is not confined to the Western governments, personal debt in the most capitalist economies is also at record high levels, and the growth of national and personal debt is quite simply unsustainable. All around the world, Government's have had to spend vast sums of money, which they don't have to save their major banks from going bankrupt. The scale of these interventions is incredible and has added hugely to the debt burdens of many countries. Just a fraction of this money would have been sufficient to meet the requirements necessary to reduce climate change.

A report[39] from the World Economic Forum (WEF) highlighted the extent to which the world was running on credit: *'Global credit stock doubled from US$ 57 trillion to US$ 109 trillion between 2000 and 2009.'* The report forecasts the amount of credit stock will double again by 2020. Most of the debt will be shouldered by a handful of developed countries. The graphs shown below illustrate only the debt held by governments and not the vast amount of personal and business debt.

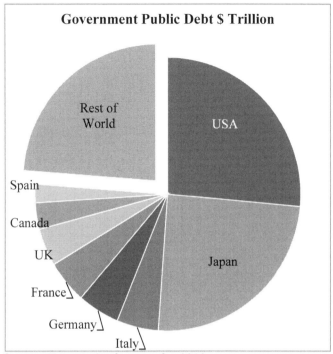

Source: Economist forecast for 2012

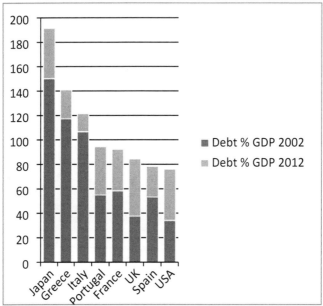

Source: Economist forecast for 2012

It is said that when the USA sneezes, the rest of the world catches a cold. Its role as the economic powerhouse of the world meant that what happened in the US had repercussions for everyone else. Now the stakes are much higher as countries such as Brazil, India and China shoulder a greater burden of the global economy. What happens when they sneeze? China not seen recession for many years and no one quite knows what will happen when it does.

The whole country is nowhere near as solid and stable as the many of us believe. As highlighted earlier, major protests and riots have rocked the entire country from the rural hinterlands to the urban centres. What is more, these riots have increased in size and intensity over the past decade. Most of these hundreds of thousands protests don't get into the western media, although the world media couldn't help but provide coverage to the major protests in Tibet and Xingang in 2008 and 2009 respectively. Hundreds of people were killed in these protests and many thousands were imprisoned. These disturbances are one tiny aspect of the general unrest experienced by communities across the country. Many in China are frustrated by the levels of corruption and the lack of democratic decision making at any level. The growing gulf between the rich and poor makes a mockery of the government's lip service to Communism. In rural areas, protests have centred on the land being grabbed for development, with little or no consultation or compensation for the local community who are often violently evicted by government employed thugs. The police service has a terrible reputation for human rights abuses, but hired thugs brought in from outside and armed with clubs have the worst reputation of all.

Each of those protests represents a spark that could one day ignite the tinder being piled high by an inept and grossly unfair government. The only thing keeping the inevitable revolution from being unleashed, is the Government's ability to keep living standards rising year on year through a consistent high level of economic growth. This is a scary position to be in when global economic growth is being throttled by a withered banking system and the increasing cost of energy supplies. The Chinese economy is particularly reliant on massive amounts of foreign investment and demand for its exports. As Chinese companies sack workers and close factories it will be faced with lower domestic demand and a desperately angry workforce that just wants to be able to feed itself. It is a telling fact, that China spends far more on its police and internal security apparatus than it does on its military.

Grey heads

To add to China's multiplying problems is its rapidly aging population; in part due to its long-standing 'one-child' policy, but also because it's vast workforce is choosing to postpone having children until later in life. The number of workers able to support pensioners will collapse in the next 15 years from 6 workers to each pensioner to just 2 workers to each pensioner. By 2030, the number of pensioners will equal the population of the USA.[40] Without sucking in vast numbers of young immigrants, it is impossible to see that the country can maintain its lead as the young dynamic workshop of the world. Just as the country starts to sample the living standards of the west, it will have increasingly transfer money from the workers to a burgeoning welfare state.

Natural systems

For the inhabitants of Earth, arguably the most important and yet *most neglected* system, is the biosphere. This is the delicate membrane that thinly coats our planet and within which all of Earth's life is contained and sustained. It encompasses all the weather systems, ocean currents and eco-systems of which we are a part. We do not need to look far to find out what would happen if the system that governs our biosphere span out of control. Our nearest neighbours in the solar system are perfect examples. Mars once had a protective nurturing atmosphere and indeed scientists wonder whether life may have once thrived there, perhaps even seeding life on Earth. Today Mars is a barren and inhospitable world, its atmosphere almost completely stripped away by the Sun's harsh rays. On Venus, the opposite is true, an out of control greenhouse effect has resulted in a thick atmosphere that not only roasts the planet's surface by trapping the Sun's warmth, but also subjects it to pressures 90 times higher than on Earth.

THE END OF DEMOCRACY?

When the biosphere first gave birth to humans as a new species on our planet, we were utterly at the mercy of the ebb and flow of the biosphere and the eco-systems within it. We were a tiny and fragile species, victim to changes in the climate and the plants and animals which sustained (and sometimes preyed upon) us. However, as humanity came of age, we started to control elements of these natural systems through activities such as keeping cattle and growing crops. As we did these things, we embarked upon a road to influencing the biosphere on a global scale. We are one of the youngest species on our planet, but for a brief time it has become our age; the Human Age. Scientists have labelled the last 16,000 years the Anthropocene Epoch, an era where we have collectively evolved from a small marginal species to a powerful force of nature, affecting the very biosphere and geology of the entire planet.

Today the impact of humans on the Earth is unmistakeable, as we have all but colonised every habitable scrap of land. Humans have had a massive role in shaping the current flora and fauna of our planet, as we have slipped out of balance with the natural world around us. Our dominance has succeeded in pushing countless other creatures and plants to extinction. This is no small feat and neither is the astonishing fact that as a mere by-product of our activities over the last 800 years, we have actually raised the temperature of the entire planet. The UK gave birth to the industrial revolution in the 19th century and since then, we have been steadily pumping "green house gases" such as carbon dioxide, into the atmosphere. This acts to trap the sun's warmth, gradually increasing the surface temperature of the planet. The biosphere has mechanisms for dealing with carbon dioxide increases, vast amounts of which are being re-absorbed by the oceans. However even these systems are simply not sufficient to cope with the vast quantities of CO_2 we are producing. Indeed the ocean has absorbed so much CO_2 that it is becoming acidic, disrupting the salt-water ecosystems such as coral reefs which support a staggering 90% of the fish we catch for food. By 2030, it is estimated that *almost all* the coral in the world will be at danger of destruction because of human activities and climate change.[41] Increased salt water acidity is also killing off another major food source for humans (as well as marine predators) as it affects shell fish growth. All over the world, shell fish are developing abnormally or simply not developing at all. For example, wild oysters have been eradicated from Washington's Willapa Bay because the acidified waters prevent oyster larvae from forming shells.

Small changes in temperature in the Earth's past triggered even greater extremes of climate than we are seeing now; with temperatures suddenly soaring or collapsing in the space of a few years. Ironically, increasingly the Earth's temperature is just as likely to cause an ice-age as it is to roast us. Melt waters from the warming North Pole are capable of interrupting the crucial ocean currents that circulate warm water around the planet. If it wasn't for one such critical ocean current called the Gulf Stream; North America and Europe would be lands of ice and snow. In relatively recent times, the Little Ice Age that gripped North America and Europe between the 15th and 19th century, was a result of a 10% reduction in the flow of the Gulf Stream during this period. Current models show that this crucial ocean current could be shut down at any moment; it is not a matter of *if*, but *when*. If that happened, the consequences would be utterly devastating. The Little Ice Age had a big impact, freezing over once mighty rivers and canals which were vital for trade. Even the great Thames river at the heart of London was frozen during the winters in this period. Year after year, crop yields were poor as the growing seasons were cut short by late starting summers and early winters, wiping out communities all over Europe from famine and hypothermia. Unsurprisingly the northern most countries were worst affected. Estonia lost 20% of its population, Finland 33% and the Viking settlements on Greenland were completely eradicated.

Land-locked glaciers all over the world, such as Central Africa's Ruwenzori Mountains close to the source of the Nile, are melting. Consequently, people who rely on these ancient water sources are facing the prospect of severe drought. Humans have pushed their planet to its limits, consuming more resources than can be sustainably replaced. We are sucking the nutrients out of once fertile soils. Most areas now farmed are utterly dependant on applying artificial fertilisers each year to keep growing crops. We are also using increasingly poor quality land in less fertile places in order to feed the growing and malnourished population. This use of marginal land raises the risk of crop failures, especially when coupled with the increasingly erratic weather patterns caused by climate change.

The 21st century will become known as the century the biosphere makes some massive re-adjustments and this will have serious consequences for all of us, especially those subsisting at the margins of survival where even small changes in the biosphere can be a matter of life or death. Despite this massive threat to our existence, none of the biggest contributors to global warming seem to be taking it seriously. With developed and developing countries alike, failing to hit their modest carbon reduction targets. In particular, the USA, as the world's biggest polluter, refused to sign up to any climate change treaties drawn up since the Kyoto Protocol on Climate Change. The protocol was agreed in 1997 and signed up by 191 countries. The USA was notable by its absence.

Future pain

It is in times of catastrophe and scarce resources that wars are fought. We should not forget the horrendous impact of the last Great Depression which spawned both the rise of our worst tyrants and the most devastating global war in the history of our planet. The terrible and destructive nature of that war was aided by the availability of new and more lethal weapons. One can only imagine the horrendous consequence of such widespread conflict with the weapons now at our disposal. One thing we should have learned by now is not to take anything, least of all peace, for granted. Before the First World War of 1914, the very idea of a pan-European war was unimaginable and again; ahead of the Second World War the European population was so unprepared for war that in the years and months before war broke out, the British Government was actually pressuring France to demilitarise.[42]

It is against this bleak backdrop that we step collectively as a people into the dawn of this new century; a brave new world of enormous challenges and risks. If history has taught us anything at all, it is that economies, societies and indeed whole civilisations are just as prone to decline and collapse as they are to grow and thrive. Just like the Great Depression and the World Wars of the last century, the great catastrophes that we face at the beginning of the 21st century are all of our own making and were all completely avoidable. There are many strategic reasons provided for why such human-made catastrophes occur, but when it really comes down to it, the real cause for these disasters has its origins within each and every one of us. If individuals had collectively thought and acted in a different way, how could the world wars have ever taken place? We cannot completely blame world leaders; their power rests only the fact that we ultimately tolerate the systems that support them.

THE END OF DEMOCRACY?

Individually we can't change the world, but we can change ourselves and collectively this is what counts. When Germany was in crisis in the 1930's it was individuals who voted for and supported Hitler's regime. Similarly, individuals in the West accumulate debts, over-consume and allow our Governments to pursue unethical and unsustainable policies. The impact of individuals all over the globe <u>not</u> doing the *right thing* has the collective impact of creating the perfect storm that is now heading our way. This storm has not been sent to us from the heavens as punishment, but is completely of our own making. The world we live in today is of our own image and likeness, are you comfortable with what you see?

The society which has become the global norm is largely at odds with people doing the right thing. *Unfettered* capitalism actively encourages and facilitates the individual accumulation of property, wealth and debt at the expense of others. It fosters a sense of the individual importance over the wider community. At its core, it is founded on the principles of economic growth. Yet growth is obviously unsustainable in a finite world. In nature, there is no infinite growth, it is *equilibrium* that is the norm. Growth must occur within the means of the surrounding environment to support it. If the growth of a species gets out of control, then the population of that species will exhaust all their food supplies and suddenly collapse, the same is true for bacteria as it is for rabbits or humans.

Humans may have cheated the system through our technological innovations, but even we have our limits. If the whole of Earth's human population consumed as much as the average American, we would need *five* Earths to sustain us. However, we have just one Earth and so it is simply *impossible* for developing countries to aspire to the American lifestyle. For the Americans, French or Japanese to enjoy their level of consumption, developing countries must consume a lot less. Instead of attempting to ration the Earth's finite resources and to consume a lot less (particularly developed countries), the opposite and suicidal approach is being taken; we are consuming as much as possible; more than ever; faster than ever.

4 ZOMBIE NATION

Opiate of the people
The collapse in church attendance throughout the Western world in the decades following the Second World War, demonstrated very clearly that those religious institutions were quite simply not relevant anymore. Today, the masses worship at the altar of the biggest and most powerful religion that has ever existed in the world to date. It could be said that supermarkets and malls are our new churches and cathedrals. For these are the places that many people in the West and around the world choose to spend their Sundays. Foregoing traditional places of worship to pay homage to capitalist materialism in the glittering arcades that have been erected in our towns and cities. If you want to escape the crowds on Sunday, go to a church.

Karl Marx, the father of the communism, famously referred to religion as *'the opium of the people.'* During his time, the age of capitalism and the industrial revolution was in its infancy. Life for the masses in industrialising western economies was desperately harsh. In his view, religion was *'the sigh of the oppressed creature, the heart of a heartless world, and the soul of soulless conditions.'* For Marx, capitalism was a terrible thing, leaving the crushed populations reliant on the solace and escapism provided by religion to get through the hard drudgery of everyday life.

I wonder what Karl Marx would say if he saw the creature that modern consumer capitalism has become today in the developed world? Perhaps he would see our western world and cry *'consumerism is the opiate of the masses!'* Unlike religion, this new system does not require you to meditate on or examine who you really are. It does not require you to have purpose or to even think about the wider world you live in. Like a morphine addict, a person gains temporary relief and pleasure through consumption no matter what the cost to themselves and the world around them. Why shouldn't you buy this or that? Why shouldn't you have fun? You are a good person right? You give some money to the person with the bucket now and again right? It's your life and it is your hard earned money, right?

Superficially, our behaviours do not seem harmful or wrong; indeed, it could be argued that we are keeping our economy growing and people in jobs at home and abroad. Delve deeper into our practices and it's obvious that our normal consumerist behaviours are fundamentally disastrous for all of humanity, let alone the wider environment and the dwindling species that inhabit the planet with us.

Life in developed countries is increasingly alien to what it means to be a human. We have lost our ancient connection to the real world around us, to our roots and to our communities. We are often so self-absorbed, that our eyes are closed to the reality of our life. Not only are we almost defenceless against the unfettered capitalist economic system, we are also active and willing participants. Individualism of the kind fostered by capitalism creates the wonderful illusion that we are masters of our own destiny, free and happy to do as we wish. The truth is, for most of us, we don't even have control over our own minds.

However, it is not enough to lay the blame at the door of those who are responsible for engineering and promoting the consumer capitalist system. Those politicians, bankers and super-rich are a symptom of an underlying problem. It is not the banks, it is not the politicians, and it is not even the capitalist system. The problem is much bigger than all of them and runs much deeper in our societies. If this problem is not dealt with, then all the debt restructuring, financial regulations or stimulus packages are going to be futile.

President Obama famously and predictably blamed Wall Street for the troubles on Main Street. At the United Nations General Assembly in September 2010, he said: *'a financial crisis on Wall Street devastated American families on Main Street. The global economy suffered an enormous blow during the financial crisis, crippling markets and deferring the dreams of millions on every continent.'*[43] It is the bankers to blame and the masses are just a victim of a greedy few! His sentiments were echoed by politicians, leaders and the media all over the world. We all agreed and were happy to direct our anger at this reckless minority. However, just like politicians all over the world, President Obama was wrong. He could not point the finger at the real cause of this global humanitarian disaster. To do so would be political suicide.

That is because in reality, the problem, the single greatest threat to our continued survival is all around us. It pervades our entire society. It is in our schools, in our parks and walking our streets. It is sitting at the desk next to you in your office and you brush past it in the street. It joins you in the pub after work and its shopping trolleys compete with yours in the supermarket every Sunday. The problem could even be you.

It is a failure of ordinary individuals like you and me, scaled up to nations that are the cause of these problems. It is the actions and inactions of the average Joe and Jane that has caused this crisis and is at this very moment striving to give the global economy the final heave into the abyss. What is most deadly about this situation is the simple fact that many of us are utterly oblivious to the role that we are playing in our collective self-destruction. To some extent we are all zombies, sleep-walking toward disaster.

It is a fact that almost all of our actions and thoughts take place outside our conscious control. Even when we think we are making a conscious and rational decision we are almost certainly not. Back in the 1970's neuroscientists were already discovering that people were making decisions sub-consciously, even before they consciously realised it. As brain scanning technology got better, so neuroscientists were able to know what their subjects were going to do before they themselves were consciously aware of their decision. In a 2008 study by scientists at the Max Planck Institute for Human Cognitive and Brain Sciences, it was demonstrated that in their particular experiment, decision making occurred approximately 10 seconds before the conscious mind was aware of it.

The fact is that no one has complete free-will or control over their thoughts and actions. Our brain's processing capacity is simply too limited to allow for it. A person so endowed with this "free will" would seem mad to us, unable to process all the information they receive and unable to make any decisions at all. Evolution by natural

THE END OF DEMOCRACY?

selection could never allow such an ineffective creature.

Modern humans are only able to function effectively because we have so little free-will. We "think" and therefore behave in predictable ways. That is why we can interact, understand and empathise with other people around us. When you commute to the office each morning, the chances are that you are dressed the same as everyone else, read the same free paper and listen to music along with the others. Your fellow commuters obey the same social conventions as they disembark from the train and surge *en masse* through the ticket barriers to their various but almost identical offices and desks. Our modern world would not be possible if we were all utterly random free thinking individuals. We would not be possible.

Without the need for expensive experiment you just need to reflect on the decisions you have made this morning to realise how ritualistic your decision making process actually is, day after day. When you get out of bed, your consciousness does not ponder an infinite world of possibilities and choice. You will more than likely do whatever you did the previous morning which was probably more or less the same as everyone else on your street. You theoretically have the free will to do anything physically possible right? But you don't. Your decision making is restricted to a tightly defined set of choices that make you feel that you're in control. Do you leap out of bed when the alarm goes off? Or do you press the snooze button for 15 minutes? Do you have cereal or toast for breakfast? Do you wear this colour shirt and tie or that colour shirt and tie? That's not true free will – that's a lab rat being offered several pathways to follow. Yes it made a choice, but only out of the very limited choices being offered to it.

Everything that we do or decisions that we make are largely made without our conscious input. One way to think of consciousness is like the way that the British government operates with a monarch as the head of state. The prime minister must go to the queen to open or dissolve parliament. The queen must also approve all legislation that parliament produces. However, in really it is just a charade; the pomp and ceremony are purely theatrics.

This is evidenced through people who have damaged or had removed a small part of the brain called the orbital frontal cortex that is situated just behind the eye-sockets. This tiny collection of cells is absolutely critical to our day to day functioning as they link our "rational" conscious pre-frontal cortex to our emotions and sub-conscious decision making. When this area of the brain does not function properly, an individual is suddenly freed of the invisible hand of our sub-conscious decision making processes that compel us to act in the way that we do. The person is now completely and consciously in charge! However it now takes hours for that person to make even the very simplest decision, they are overwhelmed by weighing up the pros and cons of each and every choice.

At best we are only capable of a quite limited level of free will. In order to gain some control over your decision making process and your thoughts and behaviours you need to exert a considerable amount of focused effort. But who even thinks about whether or not they have free will? Most take it for granted and therefore do not challenge themselves and slip into the behaviour of a zombie. This makes us much easier to control and coerce by business or government through sophisticated marketing and propaganda.

Hypnotists are well aware of the ease at which they can

make people do almost anything by tapping directly into the automated sub-conscious decision making processes of our brain. How much easier it is for corporations and governments to influence us to do things that we think we want to do. Look at how easy it is to train and control the most complex of animals that we share this planet with. Pavlov famously trained dogs to salivate on the mere ring of a bell which they associated with being fed. Animals can be trained to do anything, initially with treats and punishments but later with mere clicks and whistles. Humans are more complex but the same principles apply. Initial rewards and punishments are sufficient to coerce and control. Consumerism is fun isn't it? Buying things makes you feel good doesn't it? Being able to get easy credit to buy a new car or home is liberating, right? Why stop to consider why we are doing what we doing, after all its normal, everyone else around us are doing it aren't they?

A thinking conscious population would be able to recognise the folly of this system and the cost that it was incurring on billions around the world today and on our future generations. A zombie by contrast does not to think of such wider issues in their habitual routines. This wider responsibility of their actions or the sheer insanity of a system built on perpetual growth does not enter into their minds. They are not bad people, they are blissfully unaware people.

Those who know little of the natural world, insist that the global capitalist system is the best one because it is so linked to the concept of "natural selection" and the "survival of the fittest." The fact is that humanity is here today because we were so in tune with the environment and world around us. We did not act alone or as individuals. No the key to our evolutionary success was the fact that we acted in communities and groups. Our ancestors were intimately connected to the world around them and they recognised that their survival was not something that could be taken for granted. They knew how much they relied on working with the ebb and flow of the natural world around them. Because capitalism is so alien to what it means to be human and so disengaged from the realities of an environment with finite resources, it will itself become extinct and will regretfully take many of us with it.

The world is at the very edge of chaos and salvation cannot be a continuation of a failed system. Austerity measures and bank regulations are no better than re-arranging the deck chairs on the Titanic. The world, particularly the developed world, must rediscover the truth about the reality we live in and our place within it as part of a much larger living system. In order to continue to survive and thrive as humans, with genuinely happy and fulfilled lives we desperately need a new "system." This system cannot be primarily about making as much money as possible.

Human nature
Early economic models of human behaviour were based on people making the optimum "rational" choice. A rational choice is one made by assessing the available evidence and making the best possible logical decision. Yet these early economic models just didn't work. People just don't behave rationally at all and don't take the best optimum course of action. This failure of the models was backed up by later studies that demonstrated that half of our daily behaviours are purely habitual (lacking any conscious input at all). The other 50% of the time rational "conscious" decision making has some input but is unlikely to regularly contradict automatic and external factors and influences.

THE END OF DEMOCRACY?

Perhaps the earlier economic theories are a hangover from our long held belief in our own specialness and separateness from all other creatures. It's a powerful belief and one that has outlasted the fall of religion. Whilst we are special, we are also entirely a product of our animal ancestry. Much of what motivates and frustrates us is a heritage of our long and complicated past, honed to help us survive, thrive and be successful with the opposite sex.

We are utterly social creatures, so individualism is an illusion. Societal norms are an integral part of our decision making process. The fact is that our programming compels us to stand out amongst our peers in a way that makes us more attractive to others. Standing out is absolutely not an expression of free thinking, just take a look the array of creatures on this planet that try to intentionally strike out as individuals and stand out from the rest. Deliberate attempts at individuality in nature is driven almost exclusively by one of most powerful forces in nature; sexual selection. It is the individual who stands out (in a positive way!) that gets to have sex and pass on their genes.

Humans are a walking, talking contradiction. On one hand we are arguably zombies, thinking that we are consciously controlling ourselves but in reality following a pre-set program just like any other creature on this planet. In that sense, our consciousness is nothing more than a rubber stamp for decisions already made in the sub-conscious.

On the other hand whilst it is absolutely true that our programming exerts much greater control over us than we may we realise or even like to think; it is possible with concerted effort to consciously override our programmed decisions. Techniques such as meditation can even help to re-program our brain and alter our sub-conscious decision making processes. In other words we can train our automatic responses to behave the way that we would want them to.

The extent to which you are a free-thinking person or a zombie is entirely up to you. Before the age of six you had no conscious control at all. A five year old is effectively a zombie (without all the wanting to eat your brains!). After that point, studies have shown that on average our consciousness is actively controlling things just 5% of the time and even during that tiny 5%, it is being so heavily influenced by our sub-conscious programming that some psychologists question whether we can truly have free will at all.

One way of reflecting on the extent to which your thoughts are free or not is the amount of effort you are exerting as you think. Conscious thinking can be described as "effortful" thought, it can make your head hurt as you furrow your brow and try to solve a problem. In contrast, effortless thought is subconscious and intuitive. A kung fu expert does not consciously think about their moves, if they did they would lose the fight every time. Their actions are automatic and habitual. However the rest of us cannot automatically do kung fu. We need to *programme* ourselves to do so consciously. Consciousness or effortful thought is therefore an incredible tool for modifying behaviours to adapt and optimise them to provide an advantage. This is why consciousness has been favoured by natural selection. Yes you are a zombie, but yes you can with effort, programme how your inner zombie operates!

Making that 5% effortful consciousness count of or indeed expanding the extent to which we are consciously in control takes concerted effort. By definition, it doesn't happen automatically. You really have to want to free your mind from the shackles of its subconscious programming.

THE END OF DEMOCRACY?

The capitalist economic system is itself built upon undisciplined minds that are unable to keep sub-conscious decision making under check. As the marketing saying goes; "sex sells," and it is absolutely right. Why should a bikini clad woman have anything to do with a decision to buy a car? Or why would a topless male model have anything to do with buying a can of soft drink? It shouldn't, but the research shows that it does, simply because the marketing brushes aside our consciousness and goes straight to our sub-conscious decision making processes.

In the UK, the first female Prime Minister Margaret Thatcher was instrumental in launching the forces of consumer capitalism on the country. She infamously exclaimed *'there is no such thing as society. There are individual men and women.'* Those forces that promoted free-market capitalism systematically attacked and eroded communities and the bonds that bind societies together. One of Margaret Thatcher's main achievements was to crush the worker's unions and to rip the heart out of many communities across the UK. Even today these communities from Liverpool, to Hull and the Welsh valleys remain broken, impoverished and plagued by crime and drug addiction.

Second Awakening
Since the flowering of human consciousness roughly 50,000 years ago, humanity has been on an incredible journey. We are a spectacular creature and our achievements are truly astonishing. Yet despite all our progress we have fallen well short of our full potential. We could be *so much more*. We have become caught up in our hubris, stuck within a failing web of systems that we have unwittingly fashioned for ourselves. Our influence within the biosphere has grown to such an extent, that we

are now the stewards of our planet whether we like it or not. The direction we take will determine whether whole species, ecosystems and indeed the entire biosphere will survive. With this awesome responsibility we also have the means to make tremendously positive changes to our environment and within our societies.

As individuals and as a society we have the unparalleled opportunity to take our future into our own hands. We have a very real *responsibility* that we all bear to those around us, our family, friends and fellow humanity. Who we are and what we do has a direct impact on those in our immediate network and indirectly on society as a whole. What impact are you having? Is this the best that you could be? Are you a positive influence on the world? The fact is that we are not isolated individuals leading our very own special lives; instead we are in co-dependent relationships with other people and the environment around us. You have been since the moment you were born into this world and will be until the moment you leave it.

We don't have to be complete zombies, compelled to follow a programmed script and character role. We *do* have the ability to reflect on our behaviours and the impact these have on us, other people and the world around us. Today, even our most developed nations are at a tipping point, where its people suffer stress, depression and anxiety at epidemic proportions. Its people are trapped within systems that fulfil their immediate self gratification but fail to fulfil. We have the sceptre of rudderless and de-motivated societies that live for the here and now.

The human psychological tendency to choose instant self-gratification over long term benefits is well documented. Numerous studies show that even when we are presented with much greater rewards by waiting for a period of time, we would much rather take a far smaller reward immediately. If this wasn't the case then gambling would cease to exist as a pastime. Coupled with a free market capitalist system that encourages individualist consumerism, we have a society that resembles a crack addict, fulfilling immediate desires but ultimately out of control; on a path to unhappiness and ultimately self-destruction.

This character flaw is exploited by governments that are incentivised to appeal to our short-termism. Tragically, governments that don't appeal to this flaw in our character will have a hard time getting elected. If there is a drawback to democratic government, it is this tendency toward appealing to our own worst nature. The most successful politicians are those that can effectively use the capitalist tools of marketing and manipulation to appeal directly to our sub-conscious. Just as we all know that junk food is bad for us and exercise is good; we also know that we are more likely to put off a trip the gym and pick up a fatty snack. We know that we may feel regret afterward, but we do it anyway. It is a vicious cycle. The same psychological reasons for the Western obesity epidemic are behind a political system that is morbidly unhealthy for us. If you doubt this, you need only to visit the very cradle of democracy; Greece. Decades of people, not challenging their corrupt and incompetent politicians who would in turn look the other way when it came to the public, not paying their taxes brought the nation to its knees following the 2008 financial crisis. What stopped the masses demanding a balanced budget before the crisis? How can the public complain about the leaders that they themselves voted in? Now as an impoverished country with record levels of unemployment and a collapse in living standards, they get to vote for enslavement to European creditors (chiefly Germany) or the status of global pariah; bankrupt and cast adrift from the world's financial markets. It is a stark warning and we ignore it at our peril.

5 TRUE DEMOCRACY

Undemocratic
At the very start of the 21st century, democracy in the UK had sunk to a new record low. Only 51% of the electorate chose to vote in the UK's 2001 general election. This represented the lowest ever voter turnout since 1918, when women were not entitled to the vote. In 2005, the turnout was slightly better at 61% yet this still meant that the winning Labour Party received just 35.2% of all votes cast and was in effect given the reins of power by the votes of just 20% of the electorate! At the start of the 21st century, in one of the world's forebears of so called 'democracy', we have a system that's broken. The UK public was not simply apathetic; but angry and feeling marginalised. People saw little point voting when they are not offered real choices. In a 2004 poll, a staggering 81% of respondents thought that there was no real difference between any of the main political parties.[44] If people don't see a difference, what choice do people really have?

Across the Atlantic and democracy is no better health. The US is held up to be the very model and beacon for the democratic process. However, just like the UK, democracy is in very bad shape. Voter turnout for federal elections has been less than 40% since the 1970s. Already on its knees, Democracy in the US, UK and all over Europe has had a real kicking. We have seen a swathe of draconian new "anti-terror" laws implemented in the wake of 9/11 terrorist attack. These laws were supposedly designed to give the police and other enforcement agencies greater flexibility and power to deal with potential terrorists. Essentially the new laws have meant that the police have wide-ranging powers over people with a much lower requirement for evidence. This means that individuals can be stopped and searched, questioned, apprehended and detained without trial far more easily. These powers have in practice been extensively abused and been used to take away the civil liberties of far more people than those genuinely suspected of being engaged in terrorist activities.

In an incredible scene an elderly political activist who interrupted the UK Labour party conference was threatened with detention under the new anti-terror legislation and was dragged from the room by the police. This legislation allows for the detention of suspects without trial which in theory is meant to be used purely against suspected terrorists but can in practice be used against anyone. It was also during this time that the UK outstripped even the most paranoid of dictatorships by installing the highest level of CCTV cameras in the world.

It is because the British public have so little faith in the ballot box that they have taken to the street to vent their indignation and frustrations. In 2003 and just two years after the lowest ever turnout at the national elections, the public took to the streets in the UK's biggest ever public demonstration in history as two million anti-war protestors gathered in London's Hyde Park. Those two million people simply represented the most pro-active tip of an iceberg of disenfranchised British public who's views were utterly brushed aside by not only the incumbent party but also by the opposition party, which supported the pro-war stance. Rather than listening to the people, we witnessed an incredible act of deception as the government used a discredited and fabricated dossier of evidence that Iraq had weapons of mass destruction, ready to be unleashed within 40 seconds.

We contribute a huge portion of our income to the government to run our services and provide for our best interests as a community and their mandate should not be to spend vast sums of our money to fulfil the agenda of a few. With only the mandate of a minority of people, the UK government spent billions of pounds of taxpayer's money in the invasion and occupation of Iraq, which also represents a corresponding denial of resources that could have been spent on the pension black hole, healthcare, green energy, education or used to pay back some of our mounting debts. Not only was this war unpopular all over the world and within our own country, it is also deeply unpopular with Iraqis. The Iraqis did not and do not want an occupation by US and UK forces. The UK invasion, following a misleading and manipulative propaganda campaign on its own population reflects arrogance at best, and authoritarianism at worst. The government should be utterly subservient of its people, as a population we deserve respect and deserve to have power rightfully returned to us. The government; our government, needs to be brought to heel.

The fact is that democracy is not working. It is inadequate for an educated and ever increasingly connected 21st century population. The apathy of voters coupled with the scale of public demonstration and direct action is symptomatic of that. The current system of democracy is basic and simplistic. It belongs to a bygone era. Change has been resisted is because change would reduce the power of key players that influence the governing of our country. There have been some changes, but these have been no more than tweaks at the margins.

Bold changes are required as part of a systematic, root and branch overhaul of the way that our democracies are managed. I outline seven key changes that would help bring us closer toward the aspiration of True Democracy.

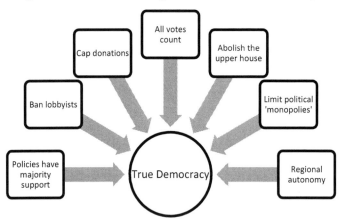

Policies have majority support – Individual laws, policies and major government decisions should not be enacted without securing the support of the majority. This will revolutionise the way that the government operates:
- requiring it to only spend time on policies that the public will be likely to support, as opposed to developing its own policies and slipping them into a long manifesto; and
- forcing it to rapidly develop new ways of engaging with the public, utilising secure internet based voting channels.

There are already voting systems like this in place around the world. The "Liquid Democracy" model is one that is being championed by the Pirate Party in countries like Germany, using the open source software

"LiquidFeedback." Essentially, it blends representative democracy (electing someone to vote on your behalf) with direct democracy (voting yourself directly on each issue). It empowers the electorate to allow trusted representatives to vote on areas they are less interested in or lack the expertise. So it gives the electorate the freedom to vote directly on the issues most important to them while delegating other votes to other individuals or organisations.

Ban lobbying of government – The government should act purely to reflect the will of the electorate. The fact that lobbying exists and does so such an enormous scale, demonstrates that it is effective in manipulating government decision making irrespective of the electorate. Lobbying of government officials or politicians should be recognised as a corrupt practice and therefore be made illegal. It is clearly anti-democratic and if lobbying should exist in any form, it should be directed at the public who must be the ultimate decision makers.

Cap donations to political parties – Funding is crucial to the success of a political party and they are therefore exposed to influence from financial backers. Clearly, the most resourced individuals or organisations can exert the greatest leverage over political parties which can unduly influence their agendas or where some parties are better funded than others, give a party an unfair advantage when campaigning. Donations should be severely capped so that individuals are restricted as to how much they can each donate and organisations should be completely eliminated from financially backing parties. Political candidates should be reliant on funds from the electorate themselves. This would quite rightly require politicians to proactively focus on the public for their support.

Remove the first past the post system – This system

results in a political landscape that does not represent popular vote. For example if there are two left wing and one right wing candidates in each constituency, the left wing vote will be split perhaps leading to a right wing victory, even if the overall complexion of the constituency were left wing. A consequence of first past the post is that the larger parties gain a disproportionately large share of seats, while smaller parties are left with a disproportionately small share of seats. For example, in the UK's 2005 elections, the Labour Party gained 57% of the seats with just 36% of the votes. On the other side of the extreme, the Liberal Democrats captured just 10% of the seats despite having 23% of the votes.

This flawed system has not been reformed because it favours the two biggest parties that between them always win the elections. This is yet another example of political parties putting their own self-serving interests over the will of the electorate and another reason why their power must be curtailed or removed entirely. Alternatives such as proportional representation, where the political make up of government reflects the votes cast is far more representative and gives smaller political groups or individuals a more level playing field.

Abolish the upper house – Ultimately, a more democratic lower house should not require an upper house (such as the French or US senate or UK House of Lords). The public should elect all politicians and political appointees should be removed immediately. An unelected upper house is common in so called 'democratic' developed countries and is the case for countries with quite different histories, but quite similar aims; to limit the power of the electorate through the lower house. Canada modelled its upper house on UK, while French officials nominate who will sit in their senate.

In much the same way as the UK's House of Lords, the US senate was deliberately designed to be undemocratic. Both houses had the role of representing the rich landowners against the common folk and block any legislation that challenged their stranglehold on the country. Even today, the House of Lords are entirely unelected and populated by an undemocratic menagerie of clergy, political appointees and hereditary peers. The fact that they are not paid is a barrier to who could hold such role; certainly not the average person trying to hold down a job. The House of Lords dwarfs the House of Commons having over 700 members, if they can be bothered to turn up.

In the US, senators are at least elected using the flawed first past the post system, but are deeply unrepresentative of the population and are almost entirely comprised of members from just two political parties. Half of the senate is populated with millionaires; showing how little has changed from its original role of checking the power the masses.[45] As an obstruction to the will of the electorate, they are undemocratic and should be abolished, as they have already been in Denmark and New Zealand.

Limit political party "monopolies" – All monopolies are bad for choice and that includes political parties. Unfortunately, just two or three parties dominate many democratic countries and this has become institutionalised.

Two political parties, the Democratic Party and the Republican Party, have dominated American politics since the American Civil War. Barriers to entry into the political process must be removed and should be configured to be as open as possible. Politicians are current drawn from a limited pool of people. Public representatives need to be more closely aligned to the populations they represent. This needs to be facilitated through financial support and training. Bypass politicians entirely if the right checks and balances are in place.

Regional autonomy – People are not a homogenous group with the exact same aspirations and needs. People are diverse and for this reason, alone greater regional and local autonomy makes a lot of sense. Furthermore, most people are affected by local government in a bigger way than national government when it comes to local planning decisions, waste collection or provision of community services. Local politicians are more likely to live in the communities they represent and be in much closer contact with the electorate. Regional autonomy increases the accountability of politicians and the responsiveness to local needs while making the country as a whole more accommodating for the rich tapestry of their population.

Future Democracy

Can we really achieve true democracy? Can we really claim to have a world run by people power? I believe so. If our Athenian forebears could create a system that was truly democratic two and a half thousand years ago, we can certainly create such a system today. While our world is far more complex than theirs, we also have many advantages over them. Athenians had got plenty of things wrong; their society had its own inequalities between men and women, citizens and slaves. Today, education is widespread and universal, the internet has made up to date and reliable information available to the masses and we have technology platforms to support direct participation in governance without the need for anyone to travel.

Even better, there are already tried and tested models of more truly democratic systems that we can adopt. By the far, the most successful system in use today, is the one advocated by the Pirate Party political movement that since its birth in 2006 has gained support across Europe in recent years and has started winning seats in elected assemblies from Iceland and the Czech Republic to Sweden and Germany. The movement's roots are in supporting the free sharing of information but they have since broadened their scope. The UK Pirate Party sets out that it is: *'a democratic political party built on grassroots support and the work of volunteers. We stand for Digital Rights, Civil Liberties and a politics fit for the 21st Century... We are a party with no parallel in British politics, wholly transparent to the public, accountable to our members and not dependent on external groups for our funding or direction.'*[46]

The Pirate Party adopts a third way between pure direct democracy (the electorate vote directly on all issues and can table motions) and representative democracy (the electorate can chose politicians to represent them) through a delegative democratic system. What's unique about this approach is that it allows voters to delegate some of their votes to others that they trust (perhaps because they have expertise in that area), while retaining the right to vote directly on issues if they wish.

Each voter can therefore be as passive or active as they want. It is completely up to the individual. It means that issues that voters feel strongly about are more likely to receive direct votes from the public, while other issues may be handed over to other representatives to vote on (for example, voters may decide to provide their vote on energy policy to a renewable energy charity). All votes from the individual are private. However, delegate decisions however are public. Individuals can revise their "vote" at any time by modifying their registered delegation (sometimes called "proxy") with the governing organization.

Conclusion
The belief that democracy is spreading around the world

and that over time we will all live in a true democracy is sadly just an illusion. The reality is that democracy is barely making any progress in the world either in terms of breadth (the number of countries that have a functioning democracy) or depth (the quality of the democracy). Any move toward greater democracy only results through the relentless and hard fought efforts of the people.

There is a great and ancient enemy of democracy as personified by wealthy individuals and organisations that wish to influence decision making. In number, they are few and so cannot win through the ballot box and so they will always erode the power of the people by circumnavigating the electorate. At the heart of almost every democratic country today is the free-market capitalist model and with insufficient regulation has created inequality on a scale never seen before in human history. The gulf between the haves and have not's provides a motivation for the few to influence government (e.g. to prevent wealth re-distribution) and the means to do so (e.g. unparalleled amounts of wealth and power).

The gulf between the rich and poor has always been one of the biggest barriers to a healthy democracy and therefore the birth of true democracy can only occur with reform of our unsustainable, unethical and unequal economic system. Our system only exists because we believe in it. I say: *'let's believe in better!'*

Thank you
This is a short book, but nonetheless thanks you for buying it and making it to the end! If you enjoyed this book, I hope you'll read my next one which will explore other democratic models that exist such as the growing international Pirate Party movement, the Swiss Landsgemeinde and the UK's People's Administration Direct Democracy party. All are examples of real attempts

to forge true democracy. For updates about this next project and future projects you can follow me below:

Blog: UtopianPath.com
Twitter: @UtopianPath

I welcome your thoughts and feedback and will always endeavour to respond promptly, so please get in touch.

've# ENDNOTES

[1] In practice this equated to about 20% of the population; men who were over 18 and who had undergone military service. Even citizens from this group of people could be disqualified from voting, for example if they defaulted on their debts.

[2] Economist Intelligence Unit (March 2013). *Democracy index 2012: Democracy at a standstill.*

[3] Paul Hackett & Paul Hunter. (2010). *Who Governs Britain? A Profile of MPs in the New Parliament.* The Smith Institute.

[4] https://www.opensecrets.org/news/2014/01/millionaires-club-for-first-time-most-lawmakers-are-worth-1-million-plus.html

[5] Dr Phil Parvin (January 2007). *Friend or Foe? Lobbying in British democracy.* Hansard Society.

[6] Jeffrey Sachs (2011). *The Price of Civilization.* New York: Random House.

[7] Thomas More (1516). Concerning the Best State of a Commonwealth and the New Island of Utopia. A Truly Golden Handbook, No Less Beneficial Than Entertaining.

[8] From that point on, the Catholic Church would exist only as a small minority religion, demonstrating the power that a few key individuals had over beliefs and practices of those beneath them.

[9] The lower classes were able to work the same plot of land, even for generations provided that they paid their dues or rent to their landlord, who in turn may be a tenant of a more powerful landowner, as was the pyramidal structure of feudalism.

[10] Jared Diamond, *Collapse*, London 2006

[11] World Bank, Accessed online: http://siteresources.worldbank.org/INTPOVCALNET/Resources/Global_Poverty_Update_2012_02-29-12.pdf

[12] "Things Can Only Get Better" is the creation of the British

pop/dance group "D:Ream"

[13] http://www.presidency.ucsb.edu/ws/index.php?pid=87751

[14] International Labour Organisation (2012), *Global Employment Trends for Youth: 2011 update.*

[15] Financial Times, *Worldwide youth unemployment*, 16 January 2012

[16] International Labour Organisation (2012), *Global Employment Trends for Youth: 2011 update.*

[17] Department of Energy and Climate Change, Accessed online: http://www.decc.gov.uk/en/content/cms/statistics/fuelpov_stats/fuelpov_stats.aspx

[18] http://www.worldbank.org/en/news/2012/02/29/world-bank-sees-progress-against-extreme-poverty-but-flags-vulnerabilities

[19] World Food Programme, Accessed online: http://www.wfp.org/hunger/

[20] *World Population Prospects: The 2010 Revision,* Population Division of the Department of Economic and Social Affairs of the United Nations Secretariat. Accessed online: http://esa.un.org/unpd/wpp/index.htm

[21] BBC, Accessed online: http://news.bbc.co.uk/1/hi/uk/7389351.stm

[22] Hall KD, Guo J, Dore M, Chow CC (2009) *The Progressive Increase of Food Waste in America and Its Environmental Impact.* National Institute of Diabetes and Digestive and Kidney Diseases. PLoS ONE 4(11):e7940

[23] Office for National Statistics (2013), *Middle Income Households*, 1977-2011/12.

[24] United States Joint Forces Command (2010). *The Joint Operating Environment 2010,*

[25] FT, *Why drought overshadows world growth*, Published:

March 20 2006

[26] FT, *Apocalypse, now*, Published: March 21 2007

[27] FT, *Region warned to address its water woes*, Published: 12th January 2011

[28] Guardian, Accessed online: http://www.guardian.co.uk/world/2009/aug/17/asia-facing-food-crisis

[29] BBC, Accessed online: http://www.bbc.co.uk/news/science-environment-11435522

[30] FT, *Region warned to address its water woes*, Published: 12th January 2011

[31] FT, China crisis over Yangtze river drought forces drastic dam measures, Published: 25 May 2011

[32] FT, World Bank chief warns on food threat, Published: April 14 2011,

[33] FT, *Glencore reveals bet on grain price rise*, Published: April 24 2011,

[34] *The Joint Operating Environment 2010*, United States Joint Forces Command 2010.

[35] *The Oil Crunch: A wake-up call for the UK economy*, Industry Taskforce on Peak Oil & Energy Security, 2010

[36] FT, *The politics of oil: Wells of anxiety*, March 29 2011

[37] FT, *Saudi oil chief fears domestic risk to exports*, April 26 2010

[38] http://www.voanews.com/content/pentagon-says-us-has-resources-for-strategic-asia-shift/1520115.html

[39] World Economic Forum (2010), *More Credit with Fewer Crises: Responsibly Meeting the World's Growing Demand for Credit*.

[40] BBC, Accessed online: http://www.bbc.co.uk/news/world-asia-china-19662365

[41] World Resources Institute (2011). *Reefs at Risk Revisited.*

[42] Jonathan Schell (2005). *The Unconquerable world.* Penguin.

[43] Fox News, Accessed online:
http://www.foxnews.com/opinion/2010/09/23/richard-grenell-obama-united-nations-speech-susan-rice-israel-washington-new/

[44] Carried out in 2004 by ICM/UKTV Endemol

[45] https://www.opensecrets.org/news/2014/01/millionaires-club-for-first-time-most-lawmakers-are-worth-1-million-plus.html

[46] http://www.pirateparty.org.uk/

Printed in Great Britain
by Amazon.co.uk, Ltd.,
Marston Gate.